CREATE
MOTIVATION

UNLOCK
THE LEADER
WITHIN

KATE TURNER

R∃THINK PRESS

Praise

'In this book, Kate gives a disarmingly honest account of motivation, in which she is an expert. If you follow her CREATE model and do the exercises in the book, you will not only understand your own motivation for change, you'll understand what you need to do, how you go about it, and why you need to bother doing it at all. A beautifully written book which captivates you at a deep level and will move you on from being stuck to a wonderful state of flow.'

— **Ali Stewart,** Director, Ali Stewart & Co Ltd, author and speaker

'Kate Turner's new book, *CREATE Motivation*, is an excellent contribution to the field of getting results not only in your personal life and career, but also at a team and organisational level. It comes down to her profound analysis of the three central questions in our life and work: What, How and Why? She reframes these in various interesting ways - I like her reframe of Why, for example, as Why bother? - which she then unpicks with copious questions and follow-on activities which are easy to digest and do. Anyone reading this book will find plenty of ideas to help improve their current situation and make them a higher performer. Of central significance to the book is the word 'motivation' in the title. We realise that although we need responses to all three questions, What, How and Why, there has been in our culture for far too long an overemphasis on the

What and How, and it is the Why that really needs addressing at this critical juncture, given what Kate calls the CR, or Current Reality (the CR of CREATE in the title). This book, then, makes an important contribution and I recommend that anyone interested in performance and motivation buy it."
— **James Sale,** best-selling author and creator of Motivational Maps®

'This book is a must-read for anyone leading a team or business. It shines a light on the importance of aligning your passion and talent to create an environment that is not only profitable but purposeful.'
— **Joy Burnford,** founder and Director, My Confidence Matters Ltd.

'Kate's definition of leadership as 'the daily practice of taking responsibility for oneself, showing up fully and continuing to grow while enabling others to do the same' couldn't be more true in my eyes. This reflects my experience of working with Kate over the years and why I relished reading her book. Her CREATE model is aimed at harnessing motivation and inspiring everyone (no matter what their job title) to step up to become a leader to deliver on their organisation's purpose. It's a model that puts motivation at the forefront, and in that way, it really is transformational for organisational culture and behaviours.'
— **Chris Sherwood,** Chief Executive, RSPCA

For my darling Maisie and Amelie. You are my big 'why', my North Star.

Contents

Introduction

How did we get here?

When I look around me and the way we work, I often wonder, 'How did we get here?' I see overwhelmed people so caught up in the do, do, doing of their role that they are making themselves ill. What is the human cost of 'digging deep' and 'pushing through' in order to reach targets? There is no focus on achieving balance when busyness is what gets rewarded. Many people just survive the week, rather than thrive. Many are not even able to replenish at weekends as they find the demands of their 'day job' overflowing into this valuable space. I hear people saying, 'There must be a different way,' but they are so caught up in the melee that they can't find the time or energy to search it out. Instead of being able to focus on what inspires and motivates them and the people they work with, they are compromising themselves to meet what the company demands. It is no wonder so many people talk about falling out of love with their role, their work and the companies they once admired.

If you see yourself in the description above, this book is for you.

Transport yourself to a future time when you have real clarity, confidence and conviction in your role. Imagine the rewards of finding harmony between your work and home lives. Imagine there being alignment between what drives you and what drives the company you work for. Everything you do feels focused and meaningful. Imagine being so lost in your work, in such a glorious state of flow, that when you emerge, you have achieved greater things than you imagined possible. You feel energised and refreshed. Stand in that place for a while. Breathe it in. See it, smell it, hear it, taste it. Imagine how you would feel about your role and your colleagues from that vantage point. Envisage how you would show up at work; how much more you would achieve; and all with more ease.

This book will show you how to make this vision a reality.

The world of work is changing

How has the world of work changed during your lifetime, during that of your parents, and if you are lucky enough to still have them, that of your grandparents? In just three generations *what* work is done and *how* it is done has changed beyond recognition. Dig beneath the surface and we also see an evolution in *why* people choose to do the work they do; in other words, what motivates them.

Much has been written about what motivates different generations, yet, as we will see in Chapter 2, motivation is much more individual than simply being derived from the generation you are born into. However, this generational view is a useful starting point as it gives a flavour for how the world of work has transformed, and along with it, how the nature of the rewards offered by business have changed too.

For 'traditionalists' (those born between 1928 and 1945) loyalty, job titles and money were the focus. With the 'baby boomers' (born between 1946 and 1964) ambition and goal-orientation arrived. Status, expertise and 'perks of the job' were, and still are, valued by this generation. Then Generation X (born between 1965 and 1980) came along with their entrepreneurial spirit, demand for greater independence and work-life balance. For them, promotion on merit, not on years served, are important. Flexibility, recognition from bosses and financial gain all became important work-based rewards. Then came the Millennials (born after 1980), our most tech savvy generation. Organisational culture is paramount to this generation, along with opportunities for collaboration, flexibility and continuous learning. Millennials regularly seek feedback and need to know how they make a difference. This generation is the first to consistently seek self-actualisation (the process of realising one's full potential) in the workplace, whereas previous generations probably saw this as something that would only be achieved outside of work. Next, we have Generation Z (born from the late 1990s onwards), who are pushing the boundaries even further of what they want work to provide for them.

In a sense, each generation has become more sophisticated and more demanding in what they want from work, and more self-aware – building on the values and expectations of the generations that went before. I see this represented in Maslow's Hierarchy of Needs.[1] As each 'lower order' need was expressed, businesses adopted policies and practices to accommodate many of them. Self-actualisation, therefore, was inevitably going to be the next challenge that businesses needed to satisfy.

---

1   Abraham Maslow, 'A Theory of Human Motivation', *Psychological Review*, 50(4), 1943, pp370-96.

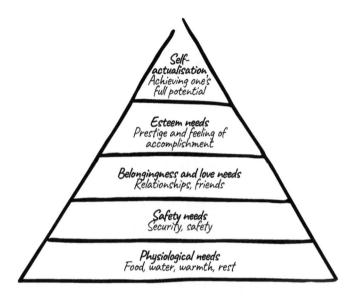

Maslow's Hierarchy of Needs

Businesses are now faced with several challenges around motivation. Firstly, how do businesses meet the needs for self-actualisation in the workplace, when to date they have been more focused on profit and targets than on purpose and meaning? Secondly, with five generations working alongside each other (with Gen Z just making an appearance), how does a business harness the motivation of a diverse workforce? Now, more than ever, businesses need to get to grips with the individual motivations of its people and not just offer blanket reward packages and opportunities. One thing is for certain, most companies are not yet meeting these challenges – in fact, they are falling woefully short.

Work is endured, not enjoyed

For the majority of people, work is endured, not enjoyed. The statistics tell a depressing story with only 13% of people in the UK being actively engaged at work.[2] Just think about that for a moment. What is the cost to our health and well-being of doing something day in and day out which we don't enjoy? Consider how many people may be dragging themselves to work they don't enjoy every day. What is the opportunity cost in lost potential, lost creativity and lost productivity?

And it's not as if we work for a short amount of our lives – for most people, work is the primary use of their time for forty hours a week, forty-plus weeks a year, for over forty years. That's 64,000 hours. The $64,000 question then is, 'How do we change the world of work so it's good for people *and* good for business?' I believe the answer lies in understanding and harnessing motivation.

Money as compensation

Most work we do is paid work. In other words, we are given money in exchange for the work we do. I find it interesting to note that the word used to describe this money (salary) is also known as

---

2   GALLUP, 'State of the Global Workplace', not dated, www.gallup.com/workplace/238079/state-global-workplace-2017.aspx [accessed 13 Feb 2020].

'compensation'. Surely, it is no coincidence that this word 'compensation' also means 'something, typically money, awarded to someone in recognition of loss, suffering, or injury' and 'something that counterbalances or makes up for an undesirable or unwelcome state of affairs'.

What are we being compensated for? Does money really make up for the loss incurred doing something that leaves you depleted? And how much of what we earn is then spent on things to compensate for what work is not giving us? Is the lack of fulfilment in work creating a vicious circle? Consider how a lack of fulfilment in work can lead to unhappiness. This may then lead to people spending money on 'stuff' to provide a short-term dose of dopamine, which leads to a need to work more to be able to buy more things.

The depletion cycle

A culture of consumption

For some people, money has become the currency for buying happiness, enjoyment and pleasure – something which they perhaps aren't gaining through the pursuit of work. If you look around you, how many people do you know that have been caught up in this culture of consumption? So many people are driven to have the latest fashion, gadget or device because it provides (often temporary) enjoyment. And while people continue to demand, the market will, of course, supply. Not only does this meaningless consumption numb our souls, it is killing the planet.

There is another way

What if we pause and start to look inward? If we were to stop the 'beep, beep, beep' of the checkout, would we start to hear the 'beep, beep, beep' of our heart's desire instead? If we take away the stuff that surrounds us, will we discover what makes us truly happy at a soul level? In the busyness of our day to day lives, could we create a space for self-understanding and introspection loud enough to be heard? And what would we learn about ourselves? Would we learn that it is possible to be happy with less stuff? Would we learn what makes our heart sing? Would we be able to go deep enough inside to hear our calling to something beyond our own immediate material needs, to something bigger? Would we be able to see the impact of our actions seven generations hence and recognise the need to change our trajectory now?

What about work? Rather than being regarded as drudgery, would we find a world where work provides fulfilment? What if companies started to measure their success not just in monetary terms, but also in terms of their impact on the world and the purpose they serve? How different an experience would this be for the teams working within them? If we are to achieve a shift in the world of work, it will need to be accompanied by a shift in our understanding of leadership.

Shifting the definition of leadership

If we look at history, particularly in the western world, the definition of leadership that has persisted the longest is the 'top down' view. We draw organisational structures as pyramids with layers of hierarchy. Yes, it is a means of organisation, but it has also served as a means of reinforcing the differences between people. The fact that we talk about 'empowering people' tells us that we have taken away their power and are now trying to find ways to give it back. There is a peculiarity of humans and their egos which means that once power is gained, they don't often want to share it.

One trend is to reverse the hierarchy and see the leader as being at the bottom of the pyramid in service to the organisation. While there are pros and cons of this model, it suggests that leaders are in the minority. I prefer more inclusive definitions such as:

'Anyone who is authentically self-expressing and adding value in an organisation is leading.'[3]
— Kevin Cashman

'Leadership is no longer about your position. It's now more about your passion for excellence and making a difference. You can lead without a title.'[4]
— Robin S. Sharma

In the words of John Quincy Adams, sixth president of the United States, 'If your actions inspire others to dream more, learn more, do more and become more, you are a leader.'

I define leadership as *the daily practice of taking responsibility for oneself, showing up fully and continuing to grow while enabling others to do the same.*

I believe leadership is not the preserve of a few but is seen in the actions of the many. To make a difference, we need to fully show up, narrow the gap between what we say and what we do, and encourage others to do the same. By creating an environment at work

---

3   Kevin Cashman, *Leadership from the Inside Out*, 2008, Berrett-Koehler Publishers, Oakland, CA.
4   Robin S. Sharma, *The Leader Who Had No Title*, 2010, Simon and Schuster UK Ltd, UK.

where every person can flourish, we can unlock the latent potential and creativity in our teams and start to achieve more with less. If we leave our egos at the door, we will start to work more cohesively, more collaboratively and more productively. We will work in a way that nourishes our human spirit, rather than depleting it. That's a world I'd like to be part of.

When we rush headlong into development programmes on leadership without first creating the space for new learning, we simply create more pressure on ourselves. By deliberately opening the gap between where we are now and where we want to be, we make way for learning to be received and to be embedded, leading to growth.

I believe there are huge challenges ahead of us. Sheer grit and determination will not see us through. We need something more sustainable, something that comes from within. *We need to align our actions and intentions to our motivations.*

Through the medium of this book, my desire is that you truly understand why you are a leader (in its widest definition) and you fall (back) in love with being one. By aligning your talents with your reignited passion, you will naturally create the environment for other leaders in your teams and/or networks to thrive, collaborate in a common cause and deliver on both purpose and profits.

What can you expect from each chapter?

In Chapter 1, we question the world of work and ask three big questions: what, how, and why bother? We show how these questions combine to serve as the blueprint for success at a personal, team and organisational level.

To bring about the changes needed in businesses, the political system and our communities, we need to change the paradigm about motivation in the workplace from being something which can be left to happenstance to something front and centre stage. We therefore shamelessly devote the whole of Chapter 2 to the subject of motivation, exploring what it is, what it feels like, where it comes from and where it goes. We'll briefly explore some of the more popular and enduring theories of motivation and ask how they can help us today. We will then look at how we can identify and measure what motivates us as individuals and how to feed that motivation every day.

Chapter 3 focuses on my 'CREATE' model. I have evolved this model by working with individuals, teams and organisations for over twenty years in my role as facilitator, trainer, coach and speaker. In this chapter I share with you how the model came about and why it is structured the way it is. Chapters 4 to 8 offer a deep dive into the model with guidance on how to CREATE the space you need to be the leader you want to become.

In Chapter 9, we turn our attention to the 'Learn and Embed' stages of personal growth and how to build habits and connections to sustain a lifetime of learning, and in Chapter 10 we bring thinking to a close and invite you to think about the next steps you will take as a leader.

ONE

What, How, And Why Bother?

Who are you?

Imagine you are being introduced to someone for the first time: how long does it take before they ask, 'What do you do?' It seems we like to define people, their identities and their worth by their job titles, but does this tell the whole story? Often the conversation quickly moves on, and before you know it you find yourself offering clues about 'how' you do your job – talking about your experience, qualifications and maybe the training you have done. This is often an effort to establish your credibility.

How often are we asked *why* we do what we do? What would you say if you were? If you were to move past a standard answer ('to pay the bills,' or 'it keeps me out of trouble') what would your *real* answer be? What would it reveal and how might it change the course of the conversation? In this chapter we explore why three questions (what, how, and why bother?) are so important if we are going to make positive changes to our approach to leadership and in our experience of work.

The dreaded appraisal

How do you know you are getting the best from yourself and your teams? Many of us were taught to manage a person's performance something like this:

- In a one-to-one (appraisal), objectives are set and reviewed. These set out the 'what' of the role – what success looks like, and what must be done to deliver the strategy of the organisation. They set the direction or focus.

- The appraisal conversation usually then turns to the 'how' you do your job. In other words, which skills and behaviours are necessary to deliver the 'what'.

When is the 'why' ever considered? How well do your team members and your boss know 'why' you do what you do? Are they aware of 'why' you work there and to what extent your 'why' is being met?

The purpose and value of looking at the 'why' as well as the 'what' and the 'how' in business was first introduced to me in 2006 by James Sale, the creator of 'Motivational Maps®'[5]. He placed all three ingredients on a 'Performance Triangle' which soon became central to the conversations I had with clients and transformed the nature of my discussions with them. (Fast forward a few years and Simon Sinek has been espousing a similar approach through his book *Start with Why* and his record-breaking TED talk based on 'The Golden Circle'.[6])

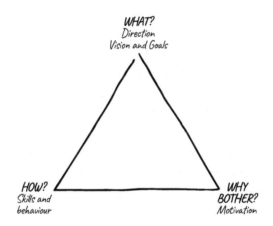

The Performance Triangle

Over the years I have built on these concepts and created my own version of the Performance Triangle, now central to the model I share in this book. I have

---

5 For more information, see www.motivationalmaps.com
6 Simon Sinek, 'The Golden Circle', *TED Talks*, 2009, TEDx, Puget Sound, Washington, https://youtu.be/fMOlfsR7SMQ [accessed 13 February 2020].

introduced one small but significant difference: instead of simply 'why', I ask *'why bother'*? This gives an additional sense of energy and movement; it shifts us into action with more gusto.

Let's take a closer look

Traditionally, asking 'what' comes first. It therefore forms the apex of the triangle. At an organisational level, this represents the 'vision' and the 'strategy' for making this a reality. It sets the direction of travel. Targets and milestones are included to ensure everyone stays on track. The 'what' is translated into objectives at both individual and team levels. Job roles and job descriptions are also identified from the 'what'. At an individual level you can describe 'what' you do – 'I'm an engineer,' 'I'm a teacher,' etc.

Once the 'what' is established, the skills, talents, experience and behaviours required to bring about the 'what' make up the 'how'. These terms merit defining:

- **Skills:** a skill is something that you are adept in. The more you use this skill, the more accomplished you are likely to become. If you *enjoy* using this skill, then you will have more motivation to keep practicing it and the chances of you becoming proficient in it increase. However, you can also become skilled in things you don't love, through fear of the consequences of failing to deliver. I didn't enjoy studying economics during my A-levels but I attained high marks through fear of failing.

- **Talents:** these are often described as natural aptitudes or 'gifts', implying that you are born with them. As with skills, you still need to use them to hone them; it might just be easier for you than it is for others. The question we're concerned with isn't how adept you are, but whether you enjoy using that talent. As with skills, you can have a capability in something that simply doesn't motivate you. How many talented sportsmen and women are there who have fallen out of love with their talent?

- **Behaviours:** I consider these to be a category of skills because they are a learnable way of doing something. Behaviours are about what you do and what you say. As with other skills, some behaviours are easier for some of us to learn than others. This is in large part due to our personality preferences and life experience.

- **Experience:** this is what is gained by doing something time and time again and, ideally, learning from it each time you do it so you steadily improve.

Finally, we have the 'why bother' which we place on the bottom right hand side of the Performance Triangle. The 'why bother' is about motivation. Why bother going in a particular direction? Why bother using or building skills and behaviours? Motivation is the energy that drives us to action. It explains *why* we do what we do. For example: if you were to win the lottery tomorrow, your capability and skills are unlikely to change, but your level of motivation and what drives you to use them is highly likely to. Winning the lottery will have an impact on your 'will' to use your capabilities. In a more likely scenario, when something significant happens in your business, your skills won't alter overnight but your motivation to use them might, depending on how you feel about the change.

As well as being distinct from our skills, it is crucial to realise that motivation is also separate from personality. Personality is expressed in our traits, which are consistent patterns of behaviour. For example, conscientiousness is considered a personality trait. By contrast, motivation is a state; and it can change and fluctuate. Therefore, it is possible to be conscientious, because this is a trait of your personality, but also feel under-motivated at the same time. In order to improve our motivation, we need to understand that personality and motivation are not bound together.

Blue elephants and stripy umbrellas

The mind is a beautifully complex thinking machine. Despite all its clever wiring, however, there is a peculiarity: in order to not think something, it needs to first think it. Let me give you an example: *Don't* think of a blue elephant dancing in the rain with a stripy umbrella. What picture do you have in your head? The one I don't want you to have!

The relevance? If you want to develop particular behaviours, make sure you state them in the positive (what you *do* want to be doing) rather than in the negative (what you don't want to be doing). For maximum success, you want to be picturing success rather than failure. To achieve the greatest improvement, be explicit. It is easy to say that you want to be 'more collaborative', but this doesn't tell your brain what it specifically needs to do. What will you be saying and doing that shows you are being collaborative?

Moving beyond the 'what'

Until now, we have tended to describe organisations in terms of 'what' they do: Lindt make chocolate; Audi build cars; Kuoni provide holidays. We are now beginning to see beyond the product or service they provide; we are looking beyond the 'what'. It is becoming important to us to know not just *what* they do but also *how* they do it and *why* they do it.

Let's take an example from the retail sector. If you want to buy a toaster, you will first find a company that sells toasters. This must be part of their 'what'. Next, you must see 'how' they sell toasters. Some retailers give lots of choice and convenience by selling them online. Some sell online but also have stores so you can pick one out for yourself as you go about your weekly grocery shop. Some go further and have store assistants specially trained up to help you select the toaster right for you. Each of these different approaches will mean that organisation employs, prioritises and develops different skills and behaviours. They each have a different 'how'.

Next, there is the 'why bother'? Why does one retailer bother to have only online stores and huge warehouses filled with stock and a fleet of delivery services to get them to your door within just a few hours? Why do other stores stack toasters in aisles metres away from your weekly shop? Any why do some retailers pride themselves on their instore customer service in plush surroundings? The answer lies in what is driving that organisation. Is it speed; convenience; price; quality; customer experience, or something else? Why does that organisation do things the way it does?

Which organisation you buy your toaster from will be largely determined by what is motivating you at that time. What you value most at that time. What is driving you at that time. It may not even be about the retailer – it might go beyond that to the brand and what that brand represents (in your opinion). The fact is that your buying decision will be based on an emotional response.

It's the same with how you decide who you want to work with. You don't just want to work for a company that has roles you want (your 'what') or uses the skills and behaviours you have (your 'how'). You also want to work for a company that aligns with your motivating factors or 'motivators' (your 'why bother'). That 'why bother' will be whatever is driving you at this age and stage in your life. Your motivators might be influenced by the generation you belong to, but they are more specific and personalised than that. It is important to develop an awareness of your unique blend of motivators – what is driving you right now.

Explaining poor performance

If the Performance Triangle explains good performance, what explains poor performance or why we get outcomes we don't want? I believe it is the same triangle, only inverted. The same three questions can be asked regarding poor performance – the 'what', 'how' and 'why bother'.

When people are unclear about the 'what' and they don't know what good looks like, they inadvertently 'fill in the blanks' and focus on the wrong outcomes. When they don't have the appropriate skills and behaviour and/or don't want to use or develop them, they use less helpful ones instead. They use a different 'how'. And when people aren't motivated to go in the direction the organisation wants them to, they will be motivated to go in their own direction. Think about an area in your life where you are not getting the results you want. What outcomes are you getting instead? Can you name your 'what'? Now look at 'how' you are achieving this; the skills and behaviour you are using. Then look at your 'why bother'. Why are you choosing to put your energy into using these skills and behaviours rather than the skills and behaviours which would get you (better) results? What secondary gain are you receiving?

Let's consider an example that many of us will have an awareness of: healthy eating. Most people know what the outcomes of healthy eating are. Most people know several different ways in which to eat healthily. Most people have a reason for eating healthily. The 'what', 'how' and 'why bother' are clear, and yet many people don't succeed. Use the Inverted Performance Triangle below to review how you are performing against a goal of eating healthily.

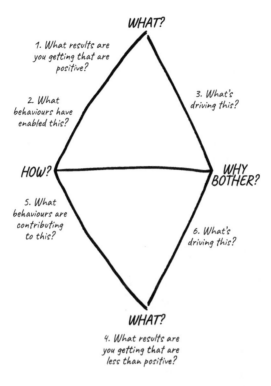

WHAT?

1. What results are you getting that are positive?

2. What behaviours have enabled this?

3. What's driving this?

HOW?

WHY BOTHER?

5. What behaviours are contributing to this?

6. What's driving this?

WHAT?

4. What results are you getting that are less than positive?

Performance against the goal of eating healthily

In the workplace, people are used to asking and answering the first two questions – 'what?' and 'how?' – yet often fail on the third. These three simple questions of 'what', 'how' and 'why bother' are the key to understanding performance. Generally, when it comes to poor performance, the motivation behind the results is not looked at in any useful detail beyond 'attitude'. In Chapter 2 we dig deeper into understanding this vital component of performance.

Summary

- The question that best describes who we are is, 'Why do you do what you do?' and not, 'What do you do?' Try it.

- Performance is made up of three ingredients elicited through three questions:

  - What? (about outcomes)

  - How? (about skills and behaviours)

  - Why bother? (about motivation)

- Motivation and personality are different. To understand someone's actions, you need to look at both.

- It is important to be clear and explicit about what outcomes and behaviours you are seeking and to state them positively. Remember: don't think of the blue elephant.

- Poor performance can also be explained through the three questions of 'what?', 'how?' and 'why bother?'. It is the 'why bother' that explains the reasons behind the actions you take (the 'how') and the results you achieve (the 'what').

TWO

Exploring Motivation

Harnessing motivation is the key to transforming our experience of work. Only through people understanding and taking responsibility for what drives them, and finding ways to have their motivators met on a consistent basis at work, will they have the energy to show up to work wholly committed, expressing themselves fully, doing what they love and contributing more through the work that they do.

In this chapter, we will explore what motivation is and where it comes from. It is through understanding what causes motivation that you will be able to dissect why your motivators are as they are and gain a different perspective on how your motivators serve you. We will outline how you can identify your motivators and how they work in combination with each other. We will look at your needs and your wants at work (both are important) and we will look at where 'Purpose' fits, as this is a dominant motivator for so many leaders.

Motivation as a feeling

To understand what motivation is, it is helpful to consider how it *feels*. Reflect for a moment on a day or a time in your life where you didn't feel the least bit motivated. Can you describe how you felt? Did time pass slowly? Did the day seem to drag? Maybe each task felt laborious and heavy. How resourceful did you feel? You might have just wanted to do the bare minimum, to 'work to rule'? Maybe you worked within the parameters of what you knew *should* be done, rather than seeing the connections to what *could* be done. How about your dealings with other people? How inclined were you to ease any tensions, or were you more inclined to disengage from the team?

If you find yourself in the company of someone who is demotivated, you'll know how easy it is to be swept into their 'black hole' of negativity. It draws you in, drags you down, and spits you out. People who are demotivated understandably end their working day with less energy than they started with. The fortunate go home and become re-energised by spending time with their loved ones or getting involved in some pastime or activity which replenishes them. The less fortunate go home, are disengaged from their families, and sink into their sofas, perhaps with an alcoholic beverage of choice in hand as they allow themselves to be transported into the land of boxsets or reality TV. I have nothing against this practice on an occasional basis or where it feels uplifting. I am more concerned when it is done as a means of escape because continued self-numbing means they will start the next day no more energised and so find themselves needing to dig that bit deeper to keep going the next day. With this at play in our workplaces every day, the cost to the economy and to progress is huge and is measured in lost sales (through disenchanted sales teams), high staff turnover (for those with enough energy to look elsewhere) and high sickness absence (increased stress levels, burnout and poor mental well-being at work).

Digging deep

It's worth saying here that just because a person is demotivated, it does not necessarily mean they are doing a bad job. For those who continue to deliver at high levels despite low motivation, it means that it is costing them energy to dig deep into their 'reserve fuel tank' so they can deliver. Clearly, unless they are replenishing that fuel tank regularly, at some point they are going to run out of energy – and either check out (through stress or leaving), or burn out.

Effortlessness

Before we move on, note how you feel *right now.* Just talking about demotivation can cause demotivation.

Let's change that energy and look at what it feels like to be motivated. Reflect for a moment on a time when you have felt truly motivated at work. Got an example? Now, take a few moments to remember that time using all your senses. Breathe it in. Smell it, taste it, hear it, see it. What does that feel like? It's quite different isn't it? Motivated people often describe their day as passing quickly; they were totally engrossed in what they were doing and lost all sense of time. Activities seem effortless – leaving you with more energy than you started with. People describe being able to get more done in less time, and what does get done, is done with more ease because they are going 'with the grain'. Motivated people have greater access to their well of skills and experience and so can draw on them without really thinking about it. Being around people that are motivated is a positive experience; we want to feel like that too. The environment is changed to one which ignites the imagination and sparks the innovation and creativity of self and others. Motivated people attract others to them; they are like magnets.

With this abundance of energy (and a self-sustaining energy at that) we can see that when channelled in the right direction, more gets done. The impact of this on the bottom line, reflected through greater sales, increased productivity, greater retention and less sickness absence is clear. The impact on well-being equally so.

What *is* motivation?

Ask a room full of people what motivation is, and you are likely to get a range of responses which look something like this:

- What gets you out of bed in the morning

- Energy

- Your values

- Different for different people

- Explains why you do what you do

- Your 'will' (rather than your skill)

- It's the 'What's in it for me?'

- The rewards (and recognition) that make you want to do something

- Your drivers

Given what we have learned in this chapter so far, we know that motivation is a feeling which gives rise to an energy. Like other forms of energy (oil, gas, electricity) you cannot see its power until it touches something.

In the case of motivation, this energy sparks action in the form of skills and behaviours.

Motivation is defined in the Oxford English Dictionary as, *'The reason or reasons for acting or behaving in a particular way.'*

This definition raises two important points. Firstly, it suggests that there is some form of exchange between the doing of an activity and the rewards (reason) for doing it. Secondly, this definition makes the clear distinction between motive and behaviour – two ideas which are often conflated in the personal development arena.

If motivation causes us to act, what causes motivation?

There appears to be no clear academic agreement on where motivation comes from. The best explanation I have seen is by James Sale, creator of Motivational Maps®. According to Sale, 'all models are approximations,' they are 'effectively metaphors' and 'their value is in their usefulness.'[7] Sale simplifies the thinking around this complex subject by asserting that motivation comes from three primary sources:

---

[7] James Sale, *Mapping Motivation: Unlocking the key to employee energy and engagement*, 2016, Gower, London.

1. Personality

2. Self-concept

3. Expectations

He asserts that these are linked to our past, present and future and reminds us that these principles are not held separately and independent of one another, but rather they interact with one another 'continuously and continually'. It is the ebb and flow of these different influences that give rise and demise to both what motivates us and how motivated we are.

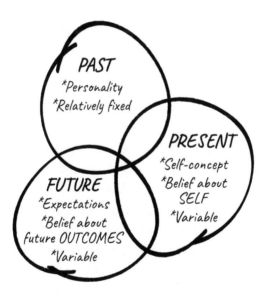

Past, present and future

It is therefore important when focusing on motivation to know not only what motivates us, but also what is causing us to be motivated. By understanding this we may be able to highlight some areas of adjustment and start to change our motivation.

Personality

It is widely agreed that large parts of our personality are shaped by the time we reach school age; if you like, they are formed in our past. The extent to which our personality continues to change, and what bearing it has on our motivation in the present and future, has much to do with whether we have a 'fixed' or 'growth' mindset. These terms were first coined by psychologist Carol Dweck, in her aptly named and widely regarded book, *Mindset*.[8]

A 'fixed' mindset is one where people believe that all their basic qualities such as intelligence or talent are what they are born with. They are fixed traits. In other words, they believe whatever they were born with defines who they are and all they can be, and so they spend their life being that person. Consider how someone with a strongly fixed mindset approaches the world and how they are, therefore, motivated. Typically, they avoid taking on challenges. They quit or give up easily. They see effort as pointless. They can resent the success of others and tend to criticise and judge others. Perhaps most damaging of all, they argue for their own limitations (for example, saying

---

8   Carol Dweck, *Mindset*, 2017, Robinson, New York.

that they are no good at maths and then using this as a reason not to improve).

A person with a 'growth' mindset, however, recognises that they are born with a set of qualities, but they see these as the foundation on which they can build throughout their life and therefore anything is possible. They believe they can create new skills, new behaviours, new attitudes and new mindsets through their choice of experiences. When it comes to the impact of this mindset on motivation, we see people with a strong 'growth' mindset embracing challenges and having the resilience to not give up. They see that effort is a daily practice, and part of what they need to do to grow. They are inspired and spurred on by other people's success and, in turn, help and nurture others. And finally, they believe in possibilities.

Consider whether you have a 'fixed' or a 'growth' mindset? How might this impact on your motivation?

The relevance of mindset regarding motivation is the hold it has over us. If you have a 'fixed' mindset, where you think that your past pretty much determines your future, then your beliefs, values and personality from your past have greater influence on your motivation. They have a greater impact on your present and future – what is possible. If, however, you have a 'growth' mindset, then your beliefs, values and personality from your past have less of an impact on your motivation and thus less of a 'hold' on what is possible.

The important piece to note is that you can change your mindset. Your mindset is formed through beliefs and beliefs are not truths; they are meanings we place on our experience of the world. By bringing awareness to our beliefs and questioning which ones serve us well, we can choose to continue believing what we always have or choose to believe something else. If you identified strongly with having a 'fixed' mindset it is your decision to stay with this or develop a 'growth' mindset. You get to choose.

Self-concept

We do not live in a static world, nor do our motivations remain static. In large part, a source of the variability of motivation can be found in the self-concept. The self-concept is 'how we see and feel about ourselves and, ultimately, what we believe about ourselves and who we are'.[9]

Carl Rogers, the American psychologist and author, suggested that the self-concept has three components: self-esteem, self-image and ideal-self:[10]

---

9 James Sale, *Mapping Motivation: Unlocking the key to employee energy and engagement*, 2016, Gower, London.
10 Carl Rogers, 'A theory of therapy, personality and interpersonal relationships as developed in the client-centered framework', in S. Koch (ed.), *Psychology: A study of a science, Vol 3: Formulation of the person and the social context*, 1959, McGraw-Hill, New York.

- Self-esteem is closely linked to our self-worth. How much value do you place on yourself?

- Self-image is the view you have of yourself. What words would you use to describe yourself today?

- Ideal-self is who you want to be or what you wish you were really like. Who do you want to be(come)?

The strength of the self-concept can be a self-fulfilling prophecy (what we think becomes what we believe; what we believe we pay most attention to; and what we pay attention to becomes reality...) so being conscious about this aspect of ourselves when exploring motivation is important.

Expectations

The final root of motivation, according to Sale, comes from our expectations and these must, by their very nature, be future-focused. Since we don't know what is going to happen in the future with any certainty, our expectations are our beliefs about the future. As such, they are once again changeable. In contrast with our self-beliefs (what we believe about ourselves) which are directed within us, our expectations are directed outwards. What do you believe is possible or likely to happen in the future? If you are seeking a potential outcome such as being successful in a job interview or bringing in your budget on target, and you believe that the chances of achieving that outcome are high, you will be motivated to do it. If you think your chances of success are minimal, you won't bother. Remember the definition of motivation also implies an exchange of reward for action: if the reward is not one you value (ie you don't actually want that job because you know it will bring more stress, or you know if you bring your project in on budget you will simply get your budget slashed next time) then you won't bother to do it either. When it comes to expectations, the proverbial 'carrot' not only needs to be within reach, but also of a variety we like.

Consider a couple of your current goals. Which of them do you believe are attainable? What are you telling yourself about them? What reward can you expect for reaching these goals? How do you feel about those rewards? How does this impact on your motivation? And on your behaviour?

What motivates you?

Surely asking someone, 'What motivates you?' should paint a perfectly adequate picture? In my experience, it doesn't. In some organisations, especially where motivation is not discussed explicitly, individuals can regard this question as the only opportunity they have to fix their pay issue. In other organisations people may feel unable to say what they *really* think because of the prevailing cultural norms. For example, somebody who is motivated by money is less likely to admit this within a charity or not-for-profit organisation. In contrast, somebody working 'in the City' is less likely to admit their real motivation is to 'make a difference to the world' when immersed in a culture where more money equals more success. (I have used stereotypical extremes to make the point, but they reflect my experience of working in both sectors.)

By asking less direct and more skilful questions about motivation, you can elicit more open and more honest answers:

- What is it that you truly enjoy and look forward to in your role?
- What is it that you find effortless?
- What else? What else?

Once you have the answers to these questions, it is imperative to ask:

- What does this give you?

It is through this question that you are able to unearth the true nature of an individual's motivation; it is here that you reveal the specific motivation (for example. 'a sense of connection and belonging is important to me') rather than the generic (for example, 'I like working with people').

You can gain an even greater understanding of motivation by approaching from the other direction and asking:

- What is it about your role you really dislike?

- What don't you look forward to during the day/ week/month?

- What tasks do you find you keep putting off?

- What else? What else?

And once again, the revealing questions:

- What is it about those roles and tasks that you don't like?

- Specifically, what is it about it that causes you demotivation and dissatisfaction?

- What would you want instead?

Through this questioning, you can unearth what demotivates individuals and what to avoid if you want them to flourish and fulfil their potential. It also gives you vital information about what they are seeking, in other words, what does motivate them. Remember, their performance may be high but if their motivation is low the energy they are expending will not be sustainable. They need an injection of motivation of value to them or they are going to burn out.

A word of warning

It is important to recognise that you cannot usually identify what motivates somebody just from looking at their behaviour. Why not? People often do things at work that they don't enjoy because they are conscientious, want to get paid or want to avoid getting into trouble. It would be wrong to presume that this means they want more of that type of work.

A common language

Each time I talk with people about motivation, they are able to come up with a glorious list of different things that motivate people ranging from the desire to 'make a difference' and 'making a contribution in the world' through to 'security', 'money', 'learning', and so on. Given enough time, the list can become lengthy and is never exhaustive because each person is different.

If we are to discuss motivation in any sensible, meaningful and memorable way, we need a common language. This enables us to articulate what we want, and what we need, from those around us. Furthermore, we become self-aware enough to be able to find those things that drive us and become more responsible and accountable for our personal motivation. A common language helps us to understand what others want and need and provides opportunities for those to be met, which in turn increases motivation.

There are only a few tools on the market that identify individual motivators. In my experience one stands out for its simplicity, accuracy, usability and memorability. Created by James Sale in 2005, Motivational Maps® is an ISO accredited, online diagnostic tool. According to Sale, only about 30% of people can identify the order and intensity of their nine motivators by themselves. His diagnostic tool has helped thousands of people around the world to identify the order and intensity of nine motivators and measure the extent to which, at any moment, those motivators are being met. The use of this common language is invaluable; it enables individuals to discover, perhaps for the first time, what really drives them. As a Senior Practitioner I have used Motivational Maps® to great effect with many clients to help them to understand their motivators more deeply.

Motivation changes through ages and stages

It is important to recognise that motivation changes over time. Different things will motivate us at different ages and stages throughout our lives. As a young person entering the world of work, you might be motivated by something quite different to that person edging towards retirement. Equally, two people can be the same age, but be at different life stages due to dependent care requirements, divorce, bereavement or other life events. These life stages and events will impact on what motivates you and so it's important to not only identify what motivates you now, but to keep asking this question – particularly during any period of change or after a significant life event.

Reward and recognition

When people describe what motivates them and they use words like 'being given great feedback' or 'money' or 'bonuses', they are really identifying the *rewards* they are seeking to feed their motivators. It is important to know this as through doing so you will be able to maintain or improve their levels of motivation and sustain them.

When looking at your top motivators, is there one which stands out head and shoulders above the rest? If so, pay close attention to this and find ways for it to be met (rewarded) on a consistent basis. Perhaps you have two or three motivators which work well in combination and for which just one or two rewards can help feed them all. Perhaps you have a competing combination of motivators? You may want two apparently contrasting motivators (and rewards) at the same time, for example, freedom *and* collaboration or control *and* creativity or money *and* purpose. When this is the case, the impact can be indecision as you feel unable to reward either motivator well. However, it *is* possible when you explore exactly where and when you need each of them to be met. For example, in the case of money and purpose, perhaps it is about working for an organisation that pays well in a sector in which you can make a difference.

It is also important to look at your lowest-ranked motivator. Sometimes your lowest motivator, that one that really doesn't drive you, reinforces something that does drive you. Let me use an example. Those who have a high desire and motivation for freedom and independence may be little motivated by collaboration. Having a sense of belonging might be their lowest-ranked motivator. When you ask them what they're seeking in place of collaboration, they might use words like 'greater independence, autonomy, the ability to work by myself'. They are (consciously or unconsciously) even more driven towards their top motivators (eg independence) because of the low importance they place on their lower motivators (eg collaboration).

Given that motivation is about where you direct your attention, it necessarily follows that those areas which don't motivate you will be deprioritised. For example, if you have a low desire to make decisions or take charge, you won't get those type of tasks done as easily (or as regularly or perhaps as well) as other tasks. This might suit your job role as you might not be called upon for those things, but it might also be an aspect that you have overlooked in how you could do your job even better. Remember, you might not even need to ultimately do that task but you need to pay enough attention to it to make sure it is done by someone else rather than abdicate responsibility for it.

Motivation and team dynamics

When it comes to team dynamics, we are used to viewing this from the world of behaviour and personality preferences. Tools such as Insights Discovery®[11] and Myers-Briggs Type Indicator®[12] are invaluable in this area but, in our experience, are not the only avenue for self-awareness and awareness of others (both building blocks of emotional intelligence). Given that motivation is the 'reason to act or behave', working from the perspective of our motivational drivers can lead to a deeper understanding of what is enabling synergy between individuals and in teams and what is getting in their way.

Needs and wants

There is an important distinction between needs and wants: 'needs' are those things which we must have to survive, whereas 'wants' are those things that we desire to thrive. In his Motivation-Hygiene

---

11 See www.insights.com
12 See www.myersbriggs.org

theory, psychologist Fredrick Herzberg uses the term 'hygiene factors' to describe factors that may not make an employee feel motivated, but that will make them feel unhappy if not provided.[13]

An employee's salary is a good example of this. We often presume that money motivates everyone, but in my experience, money is not a leading motivator. For many, it is a 'hygiene factor' (ie a need). When our pay is fair we don't even think about it as our needs are being met. It is only when we feel that is unfair that the subject becomes an issue. If you are given a big bonus you might work harder, but only for a while; the effect is temporary. To effect a lasting change, we have to look beyond hygiene factors and needs and address our deeper wants.

Each of us has needs which have to be met in order for us to survive, and in the western world, to survive well. Our wants are those things that take us beyond our needs. It is only when our wants are being met on a consistent and repeated basis and when we can rely on them continuing, that we are likely to give our discretionary effort on an ongoing basis. This is where the important distinction between needs and wants is comes into play: it's when our wants are being met that we feel motivated. Recognising and using this knowledge can have a powerful impact on team dynamics,

---

13 For a concise explanation of Fredrick Herzberg's Motivation-Hygiene Theory, see www.netmba.com/mgmt/ob/motivation/herzberg [accessed 13 February 2020].

resourcefulness, creativity, innovation, performance and productivity.

The world of work has evolved. We have moved from simply seeing work as a means of income to an activity which should provide us with greater fulfilment in life. To gain greater fulfilment, we need to understand our wants and seek to have them rewarded. This is not a demand to have them met, but rather a taking of responsibility. Individuals armed with an understanding of what motivates them are in a better place to make sure that they make good decisions to work in the right teams and the right organisations. When they join those teams and organisations, they make sure that they articulate their motivators in a way that achieves a shared responsibility for having them met on a regular basis.

Motivation, flow and the easy path

Sometimes when I am talking with people about motivation and aligning work to what motivates them, people presume this means taking the easy path. This is not my experience. To further explain this, I turn to the work of Mihaly Csikszentmihalyi, one of the founders of 'positive psychology', who was the first to identify and research the concept of 'flow'. He wrote:

'The best moments in our lives are not the passive, receptive, relaxing times… The best moments usually occur if a person's body or mind is stretched to its limits in a voluntary effort to accomplish something difficult and worthwhile.'[14]

When we work with the grain of our motivators and align them to our skills, behaviours and goals, we can achieve astounding outcomes with greater ease. A word of caution though. When you are in a state of flow, you can forget to take care of your basic needs. Many years ago, I was so absorbed in my studies and my work that I entered a state of flow only to emerge several weeks later and find I had not paid enough time to my personal relationships. Ensure you factor in your basic needs and not just your wants when considering your envisioned future later in this book.

We all have a Purpose

The motivator that shows up in the top three of virtually every person we have mapped is around making a difference, or 'Purpose'. For me, whether the 'p' in purpose is capitalised or not depends on the level of impact you are driven to have. Since most leaders want to have an impact well beyond themselves, I choose to use a capital 'P'. Purpose, then, is about

---

14 Mihaly Csikszentmihalyi, *Flow: The Psychology of Optimal Experience,* 2002, Rider, London.

having meaning to one's life beyond ourselves and our immediate situation. For some, Purpose is so strong they pursue it without attending to their basic needs and so they eventually find themselves either burnt out or penniless (or both) in the pursuit of it. For others, Purpose is something you do once you have had your other needs and wants met; it emerges once other motivators are no longer vying for your attention. For some, Purpose is a companion throughout their lives, something to which they pay attention alongside their other motivators.

I know from my work over the last few years that Purpose can be somewhat elusive. It can be difficult to uncover, discover or indeed articulate. It can also shift in form, a bit like the end of a rainbow – as you approach the end of it, it moves further away, beckoning you forward to keep going to find its hidden treasures. When someone talks about their Purpose, their 'BIG WHY', they come alive. They talk passionately about it. It makes so much sense to them – it is both completely logical and intuitive at the same time. It's a joy to behold. I also know that when people do not have a sense of their Purpose, and when they have time to think, they have a sense of looking into an abyss. When reflecting on their work and their life, they ask: 'Is that it?' As people feed their daily habit of doing, they realise they have starved their daily need for being, and at some point they are left wanting.

Bear in mind that Purpose alone is not enough – it is attending to your other wants and needs that makes the journey enjoyable and sustainable. Take two people with the same Purpose. There will be a huge overlap in what they want to achieve but scratch beneath the surface and you will see other motivators at play. One might be driven by freedom and the other by security. How they each choose to pursue their Purpose will necessarily be different as they are seeking different rewards. It is likely they will be suited to a different environment. When the 'what' and 'why bother' are aligned, you will get the behaviour you are seeking (the 'how'). That is how the CREATE model came about, as we shall explore in the next chapter.

Summary

- Motivation is our reason for acting or behaving in a particular way.

- Motivation is a feeling and it is contagious.

- Our view of our past, present and future impacts on our motivation.

- Motivational Maps® is a tool which can be used to enable you to identify what the order and intensity of your motivators are and how well they are currently being met.

- Our highest motivators and our lowest motivators are both important. They help explain why we do the things that we do.

- Purpose, or the desire to make a difference, is a key motivator for many people. A sense of Purpose can unite people to achieve a common goal. For example, charity workers driven by humanitarian principles, climate change activists driven by environmental concerns, or a belief that creating jobs and wealth can improve prosperity.

- Purpose is a higher order driver and is distinct from basic needs and also from wants. Many leaders are motivated by a sense of Purpose to effect change or make a difference. Identifying a sense of Purpose can add meaning to your work and activities.

THREE

Designing The CREATE Model

Leaders are made, they are not born

We may look at certain leaders and be tempted to believe they were just born that way but then we fail to see the work they have done on themselves to get there or how hard they are working beneath the surface. If you read the biographies of most great leaders or simply speak to the leaders you work with, they will tell of their struggles, their inspirations, their triumphs and their failures. They will tell of the turning point in their journeys, the feedback that cut through them like a knife and the stories of the differences they have made which carry them through and lead them on, higher, further and deeper. All leaders have these stories. Remembering my definition of leadership, this means all of us have these stories. These stories can simply emerge with our successes and failures being left to happenstance, or we can deliberately create them.

My story – the origins of the CREATE model

In her poem 'The Summer Day', Mary Oliver spends a day immersed in nature and whiling away her time studying the beauty around her. She concludes by asking what the reader plans to do with their 'one wild and precious life'.[15]

I look around me and see so many people being swept along by their own busyness. There is simply too much to do. Take emails, for example: how often do you feel in control of your inbox? What about meetings? Do you squeeze meeting after meeting into your day not knowing when you are going to action their results? Family lives have become so much busier too – with clubs, playdates and more to juggle, you can start to feel like the hamster in *Secret Life of Pets 2* running on the hamster wheel until you exclaim, 'I run and run and run and when I get out I've gone nowhere. *Nowhere!*'

In 2017, I got thrown off the wheel. I got pneumonia. I was told it was probably from doing too much. Then I

---

15   Mary Oliver, 'The Summer Day', *New and Selected Poems*, 1992, Beacon Press, Boston, MA.

got a secondary infection. I was quite poorly and there were a couple of days when I thought, 'Is this it? Is this going to kill me?' It was a wake-up call. The recovery time gave me time to think and several realisations emerged about how I was applying my motivators.

Until then, I had applied them in a small and safe way. My motivation had been focused on delivering meaningful changes in leadership behaviour to one team at a time. I realised that if I was going to have the impact I wanted to, I needed to find a way to operate at scale. Only then could my business make a real difference in the world. The freedom I experienced by running my own business also meant I had worked pretty much by myself. Freedom is a huge driver for me. I knew I didn't want to work within a larger company but I realised that if I was going to make the difference in the world that I wanted to, I needed to start collaborating. I now work as part of a network of collaborators.

My biggest insight was that my motivation for learning had held me back from sharing more of my skills and knowledge. For years, I had been motivated to find out more and more, believing that I didn't yet know enough to share my thoughts with the world. I was always eager to know my models, techniques and theories but I failed to own my 'magic'; what I was adding to these established models. Through my personal growth since that time I have challenged that, and the outcome is this book and the programmes we now run.

My reflections brought further realisations: So many leaders were looking outside of themselves to acquire the skills to be better. More people I knew and respected spoke of overwhelm. The way in which they were working also depleted their energy which meant they were regularly running on empty. It became clear to me that my job was to help them create enough space to look within themselves to discover what they already had: to combine their unique set of skills and behaviours (their 'how'), with their 'why bother' and align this with what good leadership looked like to them, their team and their organisation (their 'what').

This linked to another pattern I was seeing. I noticed that when I was working intensively with a group, they would talk about being motivated in that moment and at that time, but they would also talk about how the motivation (and with it the commitment to action) faded when I left the room. They needed a 'bit of Kate' to be motivated. I recognised that there was something about me and the energy that I brought to a room which infected the team with. Lovely as it was to be needed, something wasn't working if the magic only happened when I was in the room. I didn't want to be lending them my energy – I wanted them to be creating and sustaining their own. It then struck me that this was the same story I had been hearing from leaders. When they were around, teams worked well. When they took their foot off the gas (for whatever reason), their teams' motivation often faded. There had to be another way.

As I looked around organisations, I realised the answer thrown at most teams when they weren't performing as they should or when they knew they needed to 'step up' were skills and behaviour development courses. The content of these courses was more focused on 'how' to be a better leader or team member, so the underlying presumption was a lack of skill rather than a lack of energy.

The other intervention often used by organisations was about gaining greater clarity on the 'what'. Did the team have an agreed understanding of what 'good' looked like and tangible measures for assessing the degree to which it was being achieved? It struck me that little focus was being placed on whether the team members *wanted* to all go in the same direction. Were their differing perceptions of what good looked like being shaped by their personal definitions? I knew that I needed to look more closely at the 'why bother' to understand why these capable groups of well-meaning, hard-working individuals weren't realising more than the sum of their parts.

Changing behaviour takes energy

As human beings we are incredibly complex and have super-computers for brains, but our capacity to change our behaviour and effect new ways of working and new ways of being requires more than simply having or acquiring skills and having opportunities to use them. It also requires having the *willingness* to do this. I realised that we not only need to look outside ourselves to figure out the 'what, how, and why bother?', we also need to be willing to look inside ourselves to discover what these mean to us. By aligning each of these three elements to our deepest selves, our teams, the organisation and our corner of the world, change will happen.

The CREATE model is born

It was through these realisations that I developed the CREATE model – which now drives my business. The model acknowledges what an individual has already achieved and what their foundations are, but importantly, does not confine them to just these going forward. It brings together the three questions which have been central to my work to date – 'what', 'how' and 'why bother'. It also aligns what the individual wants with what the team and organisation is looking for and does so in such a powerful way that it creates additional motivation. It ensures that the individual, team and organisation remain motivated even during the tough times. Furthermore, it takes a collaborative, interdependent approach; we aren't going to be the leaders this world needs by doing it in silos. I have developed it in such a way that it can be easily used and shared. The more people use it, the more impact we will have. I hope it enables you to question your own leadership and gives you encouragement to discover the approach that will best suit you. Since I believe that we are all leaders, this model can be used by all.

Creating the space

Before we continue, I want to dwell for a moment on the words 'personal and professional development' – or, more specifically, I want to focus on the word 'development'. It's troublesome for me. It feels very corporate in language – we have learning and development teams, development days, development reviews. For me, the word feels too associated with things outside of oneself rather than with one's inner self. If you look up synonyms for 'development' you get words such as growth, expansion, enlargement. These sit far more comfortably with me.

When you think about growth, expansion and enlargement, they give you a clue as to what else is needed for this to happen: space. If there is no space, you have no room to grow in to. Even if you do manage to grow a little, whatever you have created will compete with everything else, may get overshadowed and won't have the space to breathe. Our growth as humans is little like a plant growing: if we want our efforts to bear fruit (or vegetables or flowers), we need to create enough space for the plant to grow.

This word 'space' kept coming up in my work. Coaching clients would tell me how valuable it was just to have this 'space' to reflect. Their day to day lives didn't allow for this. During 'away days' teams talked of the value of having their time and space to learn protected. My concern was, with all this pressure on their time outside of these days in the classroom, how would they make space for the growth that needed to be nurtured? If they didn't make this space, would their learnings just be filed away as good intentions before we next met? From looking at those who succeeded and made progress and those who came up short, the biggest difference was in their *commitment* to the learning. Only those who were fired up and ready to learn because it personally meant something to them soared. Those who went through the motions of learning and couldn't make the connection to their 'why bother' were floored. I needed to do more to turn up the volume of their 'why bother'.

A personal example

This idea of space has a personal meaning for me. A decade or so ago, I was speaking to a coach about my desire for a child. Nothing we were doing was working. We were heading down the IVF route and trying to fit this all into our busy schedules at home and at work. This coach said something which has stayed with me: 'Have you created a space for this child?' In that moment, I realised I hadn't. Even if I got pregnant and managed to keep this pregnancy going to fruition, I knew I would be juggling to fit it all in – being a business owner, a wife, a daughter and a mum. I needed to create the space for this child. I needed to imagine what I would be doing with my time when this child arrived and create that time now. The story ends happily, I gave birth to twins!

CREATE explained

The way to turn up this motivation, the 'why bother', is through the acronym CREATE. Before you read the detail in the next few chapters and start using it for yourself, here's an overview:

CR = Current Reality

This is about getting painfully and passionately clear about where you are now.

E = Envision

This is about enlargement and expansion. By setting out where you are and where you want to be, you will have created a gap or a space in which you can grow.

A = Align

This is about gaining alignment between your 'what', 'how' and 'why bother'. Once you have alignment, the temptation is to get going. However, there are two more steps in the CREATE model which will help you stay on track.

T = Test-out

This is where I encourage you to sit with your plans and aspirations and test-out your commitment. If your intention has not turned into commitment, then your commitment will not turn into action.

E = Engage

By this I mean involving others in your metaphorical journey so that they can look out for you, see what you are up to, and hold you to account. When we tell others of our plans and intentions we can be much more likely to achieve them. It is why I told so many people I was writing this book, as when they asked me how I was getting on with the writing, they were holding me to account.

Learn and Embed

In creating the space for leadership, we will be better able to grow and expand. Part of this expansion will involve learning, whether that be about new ways of working (technical or behavioural) or about realising what we already know but aren't using for some reason. Both are useful and both can occur in the formal setting of the actual or virtual classroom, the informal setting of learning 'on the job', or through self-reflection. The important thing is that it happens and later in this book we will explore the Learn phase further.

Once learning is acquired, we will want to sustain it and we can do this by finding ways to embed the learning. This Embed phase is the one which often gets rushed in organisations. This is where you check in to see progress, alter course and find opportunities for greater application of what has been learned. Again, we will explore this later in this book.

Take your time

The exercises you will see in the following chapters take time but it will be time well spent. Here's why:

1. In my experience, people don't spend long enough looking at where they are now or where they are heading. they rather choose to jump in with solutions and actions just to be doing something. I want you to choose the right thing to be focusing your precious energy on.

2. I want you to linger here (Current Reality) and there (Envisioning) so you really associate yourself with the pain, pleasure (or both) you sense with both moments in time. I want you to feel the emotions of now, and the emotions of tomorrow. Setting up this tension between now

and future states will bring motivation as your rational brain will see the 'right' problem to solve.

3. It will give you a reference point. If you don't record how things are now and how you see the future from your current vantage point, you will not be able to notice how far you have come when you look back six, twelve or eighteen months from now. I want you to see the progress you make so you feel even more motivated for bigger and better things ahead.

Journaling

As you go on this journey of discovery, I would encourage you to journal. It was a habit I acquired at the tender age of thirteen. When I say to people that I journal, I often get a peculiar look. Many people do not understand why I would spend time writing something which I have no wish for others to read. Others are just curious and ask, 'What do you write about?'

To help explain why I write, let's go back to the etymology of the word 'journal'. This tells us that the word comes from the old French *jornel*, meaning 'a day's travel or work'. I see this definition as two-fold: first, my journal is indeed an account of where I have literally travelled that day and what I have done. Second, and the bigger purpose for writing, is that it's a record of the travelling I have done in my mind; the rambling path of my own thinking and mindset and a record of the rollercoaster of emotions I feel.

Thanks to the work of Julia Cameron and her book *The Artist's Way*, a further aspect of my journaling has been highlighted and enhanced: that of using my diary to 'provoke, clarify, comfort, cajole, prioritize and synchronize the day ahead.'[16] I now work through my challenges ahead of time, I am my own coach and my own observer of life. Patterns crop up while I write about what I am doing, thinking and feeling, and with the glorious perspective that writing provides I can recognise them for what they are. Many of us are used to breakthroughs in thinking coming from talking things through with others (particularly the extroverted among us) but so much comes to me from my inner thinking and reflection. This daily practice is transformative.

How to journal

Pick up a pen and notebook. Even if you are the most device-savvy person out there, I implore you to use paper as something magical happens when the ink flows that just doesn't happen with the tapping of keys on a keyboard.

Write three full A4 sides. This is the length of time that it takes for us to engage at a deeper level.

---

16 Julia Cameron, *The Artist's Way*, 1995, Pan Books, London.

Just write. No one else is going to see it, so no need to self-edit. Use a stream of consciousness to capture every thought even if you end up writing, 'I don't know what else to say. I am noticing the aeroplane flying overhead and now a car passing...' The point is that you are still writing, becoming more present to you and all that you are. As your mind wanders back to the now, you will start to capture the now of you. From that place you will have a window into the world of what is really going on: Self-doubt (your 'gremlins') gets to speak; ambition gets to speak; guilt gets to speak; excitement gets to speak...

Resist re-reading your journals for several weeks. When you do go back, look for the themes that are emerging. Notice how you are changing. Observe what patterns are pushing you forward and holding you back. Use your curious mind when reading, not a judgmental one. Have no expectation of what you will read: read it like it is new to you – this perspective will truly be a revelation to you.

Write daily. Some suggest that the best time of day for journaling is in the first few moments when you wake – when you are in that dreamlike stage of the day. This is the time before the gremlins have had time to wipe the sleepy dust from their eyes. For now, I just want you to write, so just do it at whatever time of day you can and do it daily. When you've got the journaling bug, start seeing whether a different time of day works better for you. Happy writing!

Summary

- To fulfil your full potential and show up as the best version of yourself, start by being deliberate.

- In order to grow, we need to create space to do so.

- CREATE stands for:

  - Current Reality (CR)

  - Envision (E)

  - Align (A)

  - Test-out (T)

  - Engage (E)

- A transformative habit which leads to less stress and more creativity and growth is journaling. Get writing.

FOUR

CReate: Current Reality

'An accurate, insightful view of current reality is as important as a clear vision.'[17]
— Peter Senge

When working with personal growth, it is tempting to start with the end in mind. This is what pulls us forward and takes us to a more expansive space. I do want you to go there in your mind, but not yet. We need to check in on your starting place. In this chapter we explore the first stage of the CREATE model – Current Reality – and explain why it is so important to begin here.

---

17 Peter Senge, *The Fifth Discipline*, 2006, Random House, London.

What do you do?

Does that question fill you with dread, or with excitement? Go ahead, answer it now in your head. What words spring to mind?

Chances are your words include a range of information about what you do (for a living), where you live or hail from, whether you are married or not, whether you have children or not. The list could be huge. Your answer to that question is also likely to be different in different contexts. For example, what if your new boss was asking you? What about a new contact you are wanting to impress to secure work? A parent of one of your child's friends? Or maybe an introduction made at a party? Would it matter which party? How we describe ourselves necessarily changes depending on the context in which we are asked. What we share is relevant to the situation. We have many aspects of ourselves we can share. Different layers.

As you read and do the activities suggested in the next few chapters, I would like you to keep seeing yourself from these different aspects or layers. I invite you to see yourself from deep within. Who are you *really*? Each one of us, to some extent, carry a mask around that shows a different version of who we are to the outside world. Who is behind your mask? Who was that person once, and who is that person now; the 'good' and the 'not so good'? What qualities, aspirations, skills, behaviours and motivations have you collected along the way and which ones have you let go of? For those aspects you have kept, are they serving you well? For those that you have let go, has that been a help or hindrance to where you find yourself today? Take a while to ponder on these questions before you read on. They will help you to open your mind to the wholeness of you. Your answers will certainly be something that you can journal on.

A constant theme over the next few chapters is the message that the more you use the activities in this book, the more you will get from it. After all, there is a huge difference between thinking about going to the gym, and actually going to the gym. If you are one of those that prefer to read the whole of this book (to get your bearings) and then do the work, equip yourself with some stickies and a pen so you can mark up the activities and make it easier for you to find them again. Whatever you do, do the work – you get the message.

Take what's useful, leave what's not

There are so many choices to make over our lifetime. So much knowledge to gain. So much experience to develop. Hopefully we try and take what is useful and leave what is not, but it is my experience (both personally and from working with clients) that some of what is not useful still sticks to us like burs. You know the ones – you might be able to pull off the main part but little tiny parts of them still claw their way into your clothes. Through the course of this chapter, we will get to grips with some of these burs and lessen their hold on you. In doing so, *you* will shine through.

Equally, you will have aspects of yourself that you possibly take for granted as they are just so 'you'. You have qualities that others greatly admire. You have ways of working which come so naturally to you that you barely notice you are using them. Now is the time to highlight these aspects. It is important to fully claim these gifts, skills and approaches as yours. Whether you are a religious person or not, it might be helpful to think of them as 'God-given' as they are gifts that seem to be intrinsic to you from birth. To not let them shine would be a disservice; imagine if Elvis had never used his gift!

I invite you to hear what your inner dialogue is telling you that you 'ought' to write down and that you 'should' write down, plus what you wish you 'could' write down and what you wish were true. All that noise is telling you something about your personality, your self-concept and your expectations. We will be exploring gremlins and limiting self-talk later in the book.

Discovering your Current Reality

In the next few pages, I invite you to unpack, explore and discover the reality of your current situation. In order to get the full picture, I will be asking you to consider your role(s) in the team(s) within the organisation(s) you work for, even if that organisation is your own business. At this stage we are just telling it as it is. No need to judge or analyse. Just follow the exercises and write down what feels true for you today. In Chapter 6 (Alignment) we will be using the output from this chapter and Chapter 5 (Envision) and pulling it all together.

How to record your answers

The questions set out below require lots of thinking and reflection. For this reason, they are well suited to a coaching or buddy conversation, a stream of consciousness in your journal or a brain-dump on paper. Choose whatever suits you or combine a couple of methods to reveal more answers. Since the questions are based on the Performance Triangle, some people find putting this diagram in the middle of a flip chart useful (see illustration). You will have lots to write so just use a normal pen to record your answers. Better still, record your answers on lots of sticky notes so you can move them around on the flip chart.

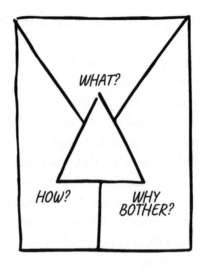

Using the Performance Triangle on a flip chart

Whatever method you choose, have some thoughts written down somewhere so you can use them later. Your thoughts don't need to be organised; it's more about giving voice to this version of you. As you start digging, you will inevitably unearth some less than positive results. Record these in a separate place, perhaps drawn as the inverted Performance Triangle. Have this information to hand when you reach the Test-out stage of the CREATE process to make sure you overcome these unhelpful ways of working in the future.

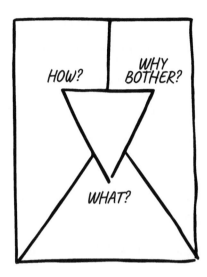

Inverting the Performance Triangle

Your 'What'

First, let's explore what is happening now and view this from the 'what'. The following categories and questions are designed to make you think. You don't need to answer every question.

Consider yourself

- What do you do for a living?

- What roles do you have? You might be a leader, a team member, an employee, a business owner, etc.

- What are your current goals and/or objectives?

- What are your recent achievements?

- How do you describe what you do?

- What does success look like to you right now?

- How successful are you? How do you know?

- Who do you regard as your peers?

- How do others describe what you do (not how you do it)?

- What are the 'big ticket' items on your to-do list?

- What other roles do you have outside of work right now? You might be a parent, volunteer, sports team member, etc.

Consider the teams you work in

Now think more broadly and consider your role in the teams you are working in. If you work in more than one team then separate out your answers for each team:

- What's your role in this team?

- What additional goals and/or objectives do you have as a result of being a member of this team?

- What has your biggest achievements in this team been?

- What are you most proud of having achieved as a member of this team?

- What do other people in this team rely on you for?

- How successful are you in this team?

- What are the big challenges you face by being a member of this team right now?

Consider the organisation you work for

Finally, consider your role in the organisation that you are working for:

- What's the 'what' of the organisation? What does it do?

- Which part of that are you responsible for achieving?

- What role do you see this organisation having in society / the world at large?

- What does it see as success?

- What are the biggest challenges facing the organisation right now?

- How does this impact you?

Your 'How'

How do you do what you do? Here we are looking at the skills and behaviours you use which enable you to deliver the 'what'. If you draw a blank on this, reach out to others to help you.

Consider yourself

- What are your key skills?

- What are your key talents?

- What 'life' experience do you have?

- What's your key area of knowledge?

- What's your 'magic power'?

- What can people rely on you for?

- What behaviours come easily to you?

- How would you describe your style as a leader?

- How do others describe the way in which you work?

Again, if you come across less than desirable ways of working, such as things you do that derail you or what you perceive as weaknesses, note them down separately.

Consider your role in teams

What additional skills, behaviours, talents and/or knowledge do you use in this team role that you don't use elsewhere? (If you don't work in an actual team, think more laterally about who you work alongside.)

- How do you contribute to the team's 'magic power'?

- How would you describe your style as a team member?

- What do other team members rely on you for in this role?

- Overall, what is the team's preferred way of working? How does this impact on you?

- What, if anything, is different about the way you show up in this team than when you are working elsewhere?

Consider the organisation you work for

- What key skills does this organisation value? Do you have these?

- What talent does it attract and nurture? Do you have these?

- What's special about the way this organisation does what it does? How does this impact on how you do what you do?

- What key cultural traits impact how you do what you do?

Your 'Why bother'

Next, we come on to the motivation piece – the 'why bother'. I have already mentioned that motivation changes at different ages and stages of life. What drove you a few years ago may not drive you now. Working in the present tense, answer the following questions.

Consider yourself

- Why do you do what you do?

- What do you love doing?

- What gets you in flow?

- How supported do you feel in what you do?

- How challenged do you feel in what you do?

- How positive are you about making changes?

- How confident do you feel about what you do?

- What motivates you?

- Do you feel you are in an upward spiral of motivation, a downward one, or holding steady?

- To what extent do you have a fixed or growth mindset?

- What words describe how you feel about your work right now?

- How motivated are you?

Consider the team

When you answer the following questions, notice what impact working in this team has on your 'why bother':

- What drives this team? How does this impact you?

- When do you feel most in flow in this team?

- How supported do you feel in this team?

- How challenged do you feel in this team?

- How does this team view change? How does this compare to you?

- How motivated is this team right now? How does this compare to you?

- How motivated are you being a member of this team?

Consider the organisation

When you answer the following questions, notice what impact working for this organisation has on your 'why bother':

- What drives this organisation?

- What is its purpose?

- What are the key rewards and forms of recognition given?

(Completing a Motivational Map® with an accredited organisation such as Motivational Leadership as you work through this stage of the process is highly recommended as it will further assist you in gaining a current picture of what drives you.)

Reflect and revisit

That's the Current Reality piece almost done. It's a good idea to come back to this document a few times over the space of a week or two. You will think of more things as you let your less conscious mind search for the answers. It would also be worth getting input from others – particularly on your 'how' – since other people may well see things that you do not. This will help reveal aspects of yourself that you may take for granted and aspects of yourself that you are blind to. Both can be useful.

Which version are you working from?

In this digital age we are all used to receiving new versions of software and operating systems enabling new ways of working, but our personal growth is more subtle, and we can forget to acknowledge that we are working from progressing versions. Through completing this exercise, I hope you will start to see the *current* version of you; where you are *now*. I find that many people operate from an old, outdated version of themselves. Some focus so much on the skills and work they are doing now that they fail to bring with them the jewels of experience from previous roles. Others are still listening to feedback they received years ago about what they were good at then and failing to claim the new skills they have since acquired. To fully show up, I need you to look across the *whole* of your life and powerfully combine all versions; taking what's useful and leaving what's not. You will see things quite differently when you begin operating from this new vantage point.

MONICA: A CASE STUDY

Monica was a middle manager when she attended an in-house programme on leadership that we were running for a client. Monica was capable, well respected and led a team who were widely regarded as delivering well. The programme was in full swing and her contributions had been useful – encouraging other colleagues by sharing her experience with them

83

and often being able to bring to life the models and theories I was using. She held back in one of the breaks to speak to me, looking troubled. She explained that, while she had enjoyed the programme and much of it had resonated with her own experience, it wasn't giving her anything new to do with the team. She had already set out a vision of what success looked like and had been holding her team accountable to it. They were delivering well. They felt empowered and were now coming up with ideas and recommendations on how they could improve what they delivered. I sensed she was feeling redundant. Now that she had helped the team to achieve her original vision, what was her role? They didn't seem to need her much these days. She expressed that she was finding her role with the team so minimal that she didn't feel she could justify the high salary she was on.

Monica was in the all too familiar position of the successful manager, namely:

- She had achieved what she had originally set out to do. The team had achieved her 'vision' – the 'what'.

- The management skills and behaviours she once struggled with were now second nature to her. She was effortlessly employing her 'how'.

- Given her success, she thought she should be feeling motivated, but she wasn't. She knew she was motivated by making a difference but she no longer felt she was making a personal difference as it was now being done through the team. She was also motivated by expertise but felt that this wasn't being tested as much as it once was.

It was easy to see why she felt a bit despondent. I asked her some of the questions from the Current Reality list and encouraged her to challenge how she saw herself *now*. She quickly recognised that her idea of what success looked like was being viewed from the vantage point of an 'old' version of herself. She had not set out what good looks like *now*. She also recognised she had not fully embraced her newfound talents and took them for granted rather than fully valuing them. In exploring some of the other roles she had in the company, she started talking about her work on cross-directorate projects. She realised that she had seen this work and the challenges it presented as her own challenges so she had been protecting her team from them. She had been handling the inter-departmental politics and she had been developing a realistic plan and budget alone as she saw herself as the one who could best represent this function in these cross-functional discussions.

The penny dropped. She needed to fully step into her established role of the leader of a successful team and work with them to step up to their next level of success. That success would require them to work more cross-departmentally. To do this successfully, she needed to look at the next stage in the CREATE model – Envision. This would start with her own new vision of success and then move on to involving her team. As for the programme she was attending, she realised she had been viewing the material I was sharing from an old version of herself rather than seeing the material with fresh eyes from the vantage point of the new version. She was able to recalibrate what we covered and realised she could take her understanding of what she thought I had been saying to a deeper level.

Review and reset

Given the number of questions you have answered and deep thinking you have done, you may now have pages of notes or a very full flip chart. Now you need to make sense of it. A simple way to do this is to reach for a highlighter pen and identify key words and phrases that give you a strong sense of who you are now. If you have used sticky notes, start to sort them into themes or common thoughts. Who are you today? What words do you notice as you scan your pages or flip chart?

Our personal growth is like a vista of mountains; it's only when we climb them that we get a clearer view of what lies beyond. Your Current Reality is one of these mountains. When you started your journey, you carried a whole bunch of skills, experience and behaviours in your rucksack, ready to be used when called upon. Along the way you collected more skills and experience until, finally, you reached the top of this mountain, now fully laden. Linger here a while. Fully appreciate the journey you have been on. Truly acknowledge your skills, successes and how you feel, for soon I will be asking you to contemplate the next stage of your journey. Some of those skills have served their purpose and you will no longer need to carry them. Like a well-thumbed reference book, you now know its entire content. If you need the content, it will be there for you in that super-computer in your head but you don't need to carry the book any longer. Prepare to make way for new learning.

Accepting poor results

If you have completed an inverse Performance Triangle, now is a good time to review it. What do you notice? What are the poor results you have been getting and what has driven you to these? What are the unhelpful skills and behaviours you would like to leave behind? What could you do in the future to meet your needs and wants from an overt place, rather than a place of secondary gain? The aim for now is to be aware of these behaviours, motivators and habits. The next chapter will give you an opportunity to redirect them.

Write your story – connect your dots

'You can't connect the dots looking forward; you can only connect them looking back-wards. So you have to trust that the dots will somehow connect in your future. You have to trust in something – your gut, destiny, life, karma, whatever. This approach has never let me down, and it has made all the difference in my life.'[18]
— Steve Jobs

An exercise I encourage you to do is to look back over your life and connect the dots. The things you

18 Steve Jobs, commencement address delivered at Stanford University, 12 June 2005, https://news.stanford.edu/2005/06/14/jobs-061505 [accessed 13 February 2020].

do and experiences you have throughout your life shape who you are and lead you to your destiny. As I look back through my life to date it now makes sense. Disappointments and apparently wrong turns at the time have made me who I am. Opportunities helped me forge forward. From this foundation, I am now able to trust that these experiences will connect to my future.

Let me share my story with you to show you what I mean.

I really enjoyed school. I loved the learning. I loved the teachers. I loved the accolades of doing well. There was no doubt in my mind I would go to university: not because my family had been or my friends were going, but because I thought that was what you needed to do to be successful. I thought achievement was measured in good exam results, having a 'profession' and earning good money. At this point in my life, my 'what', 'how' and 'why bother' looked like this:

- What: get good exam results

- How: study hard

- Why bother: I loved learning and want to be valued by others

For a period, the profession I thought I would pursue was law. I thought that by becoming a lawyer I would *be* someone. Interestingly, as the day approached for me to select which universities to go to, a small voice inside me said, 'No'. I realised that while I wanted to be successful, I couldn't imagine myself enjoying studying law and for me, enjoying what I was learning was paramount. Fortunately, I found out that I could study other subjects and then switch to law later. That appealed, so I chose two subjects which I really loved – history and politics. The history part was always social economic history (and more concerned with the 98% of the population rather than the top 2%) and the politics reflected something in me which was screaming, 'Why does it have to be like this?' Are you seeing my dots connecting yet between this and my view of leadership? I didn't know that then...

I went to Warwick University. I remember many a time when climbing the stairs to the history department, a part of me wanted to turn right at the top (to the psychology department) rather than continue left to the history department. It didn't make sense to me at the time and it wasn't a big enough calling for me to act on it. What use would psychology be to me? Little did I know.

I studied hard, got my obligatory degree and by that point becoming a lawyer was a distant memory. I didn't know what I wanted to do so I got swept up by the 'milk-round' and found myself applying for accountancy jobs (which was bizarre as I really did not enjoy numbers), a 'profession' my ego was telling me I should pursue. Needless to say, the 'milk-round' spat me out. I left university, went home and just picked up a job at our local big employer. I was an admin assistant in an insurance firm. There I noticed I wanted to excel in everything I did. I wanted to soak up the knowledge and work hard. I moved on to become a pensions administrator in an actuarial company. Once again, there was an opportunity to study and I found I threw myself fully into it even though I didn't much like the subject (too technical, more numbers). My love of learning was burning bright. This was still my 'why bother' but I was confused on which 'how' to follow and which direction to go in (my 'what').

Before long I realised that pensions admin was not for me. Sitting all day in a room full of actuaries when you are an extrovert is a hard thing to do. On the outside, I was able to do a good job, but on the inside, I was screaming. I felt a need to do something that mattered. This came up in the guise of a Human Resources (HR) role in the oil and gas sector. I saw HR, or rather the people it served, as central to the business and that's where I wanted to be. I didn't know it then, but my sense of purpose was growing. (Notice how my 'why bother' was changing and influencing my 'how' and 'what' choices.)

Next followed several years working my way around different functions in the HR team – recruitment, employee relations, international assignments – oddly, focusing on employment law and international tax. My love of learning was still huge and I studied hard for my professional exams. I realised that I was now in a career and not just a job. It was while I was working at this company that I was lucky enough to experience the good, the bad and the ugly of leadership and through this became fascinated in what leadership is and isn't.

I then decided to move to a company and try my hand at being an HR Director. I remember arriving at the new company in my expensive new suit, earning a salary my eyes boggled at. I sat down in my new office (not quite oak panelled but it felt like that) and I caught sight of my reflection in the glass door – I felt I had arrived. About the same time, I remember feeling what a fraud I was. What did I know? I have since found that the time of greatest growth is also the time when imposter syndrome rears its ugly head.

Turns out the role wasn't as advertised. My first task was to make a huge raft of staff redundancies. I learned big lessons at this company, and they were far from what I thought I would learn. I learned from my own shortcomings. I learned that having a good technical knowledge isn't enough. I learned being technically right and doing the right thing are not necessarily the same thing. It seemed that my formative years in HR had been about technical knowledge and not about people. I quickly needed to learn what made people tick. This was when a psychology degree would have been useful.

I learned that the behaviours at the top of organisations have a huge ripple effect on the culture, performance and atmosphere of the whole organisation. When it is negative and not working, the organisation is negative and not working. After months of trying to work out what to do, I finally called in an external company to help mend the team. That's when my eyes opened. It was then that I realised my calling. I wanted to enable people to be the best they can be. To do that, people needed help to build self-awareness and awareness of others – basically build Emotional Intelligence. This was the early noughties so Daniel Goleman's work with the concept of Emotional Intelligence was only just becoming known[19]. I remember reading an article about leadership that I was given and finally feeling awake at the realisation that I could *choose* what type of leader I wanted to be.

As the months passed, I realised I was in the wrong company. My desire for learning and making a difference was not being nourished. I remember climbing the stairs to my office, once again wishing I could turn in a different direction. I remember how heavy my legs felt as I ascended the stairs knowing that I would not be giving of my best today nor would I be enabling that in others. I remember dragging myself into work, just thinking of the money (I was still being paid well), but it felt like a small part of me died each moment I was there. I remember being on my

---

19 Daniel Goleman, *Emotional Intelligence: Why it can matter more than IQ*, 1996, Bloomsbury, London

morning commute into London, noticing the time on the clock at Waterloo station – and wishing it was nine hours later and I could go home. I was wishing my life away. Soul destroying. Mind numbing. Pointless. Something had to change. Whatever came next had to fulfil my desire for learning, for making a difference, and the growing yearning for the freedom I was feeling.

The answer came sometime later, when I set up my first business providing training and coaching to senior teams. It's probably no surprise that I was attracted to work in the field of motivation; I was curious to understand why people do what they do. I was introduced to Motivational Maps® in 2006 by Steve Jones and once again my eyes were opened. I finally had the language to explain what had been driving my decisions to date. In my early career it had been the lure of prestige and power and accolades. It was what others (or what I thought others) were telling me about what success meant – power, prestige, status, public recognition, money. These were 'should dos' and didn't sit comfortably with me.

A love of learning has been a constant throughout my life and I very much hope it never changes. Freedom is also very important to me. My version of freedom is about being able to fully self-express, to feel free to spread one's wings (rather than have them clipped by the ambitions or insensitivities of others). For me, freedom allows me the space to breathe, learn and grow.

And finally, purpose. At first my purpose was indeed with a small 'p'. I needed to know that what I did contributed in some way; that what I did had a positive impact on someone or something. Now it is Purpose with a big 'P'. I have a strong vision: inspiring a generation of leaders to ignite their talents and motivators and those of the people they work with to make a positive difference in the world.

This is an account of my first dozen years or so in work and explains my move from seeing work as a job, to a career and finally, a wonderful calling. The latter came through enabling my motivators to be well met and aligned. Before you read on, what's your story? Take a minute to join the dots of your own journey so far.

Summary

- Your Current Reality is best viewed from exploring your 'what', 'how', and 'why bother'.

- Own your 'God-given' or intrinsic gifts.

- Your identity is influenced by the teams and organisations you work with.

- You can learn much from poor performance – look at your inverted Performance Triangle.

- Make sense of your journey by joining the dots.

- Fully embrace the latest version of you.

FIVE

crEate: Envision

'What you envision in your mind, how you see yourself, and how you envision the world around you is of great importance because those things become your focus.'[20]
— Eric Thomas

For any of us to grow, just like plants, we need space. I believe one way to create that space is to see the gap between where we are now (Current Reality) and what we want to become. Having done the work in the last chapter, you are now standing on solid ground regarding your Current Reality. You know who you now are. From this vantage point, at the top of this mountain, you can envision your future. This chapter will show you how.

---

20 Eric Thomas, https://etinspires.com/home [accessed 13 February 2020].

The power of visualisation

I have always been a fan of the quote 'if you can dream it, you can become it'.[21] The value of future-gazing is not simply about knowing where to focus your energies going forward, although it will naturally result in this. It's not simply that by freeing yourself of the 'here and now' you will feel motivated and inspired by what could be; although this is also likely to happen. The real value of envisioning lies in the neuroscientific evidence that your brain is unable to distinguish between what is real and what is imagined. Numerous studies have shown that when you imagine, or trick your brain into a state, it starts to make physical changes in your body as if this imagining were true.[22] A simple version of this can be demonstrated by imagining your favourite food. Imagine it right there in front of you now, lifting it to your lips, biting into it and savouring the taste. Are you salivating at the thought? That's your imagination in action. Wonderful, isn't it? Furthermore, when you imagine yourself doing something, you get better at it and you are more likely to succeed. That's everything from weight loss or becoming an Olympic medal winner to running a multi-million-pound business.

---

21 This quote is widely attributed to William Arthur Ward although the first use of the quote is unknown.

22 A J Adams, 'Seeing is Believing: The Power of Visualization', *Psychology Today*, 2009, www.psychologytoday.com/us/blog/flourish/200912/seeing-is-believing-the-power-visualization [accessed 13 February 2020].

How do you dream up a future vision? People do it in lots of different ways and they tend to fall into two camps. One camp is to leap to the end point (to dream). The other camp is to start from where you are now. We will look at both. Whichever way you choose (you can choose either or both), by the end of this chapter you should see in your mind's eye a clear picture of your future self.

Getting to know your gremlins

When some people start to dream about their future, the first thing they encounter are their gremlins. These gremlins are the narrators in their heads who chat to them incessantly as they are trying to do something (some people call them the 'chattering monkeys'). They say things like:

- You aren't good enough

- You'll never be able to do that

- Who do you think you are?

- You'll fail

- People will laugh at you

They produce an eloquent stream of negative self-chatter that has the potential of keeping you down and not enabling you to fulfil your full potential. Whatever you want to call them or refer to them as, you'll know what I am talking about. I've yet to come across a person who doesn't experience interactions with these pesky gremlins. They have influenced you since an early age, reciting well-versed limiting beliefs in such a familiar way that maybe you interpret these beliefs as truth. The question is, what influence will they have on you going forward? It is time to check out your gremlins.

Gremlins and self-concept

Let's start by assessing your self-concept, that piece of motivation that we talked about in Chapter 2:

- What do you believe about yourself today?

- What do you feel about yourself?

- What do you think is possible for you to have happen in your life?

As you journal your answers to these fundamental questions, consider where any limiting beliefs come from. How they are serving you now? Which ones have outlived their usefulness?

Now start thinking about what alternative *empowering* beliefs you could replace them with. Have a play with some new ones. What's the opposite of what your gremlin would have you believe? Commit to seek evidence that your new beliefs hold more truth for you than the rubbish your gremlins spout. Embed these new beliefs. Nourish them. Let them become part of your narrative going forwards.

Freezing the gremlin

Gremlins can intrude on your thinking when you least want them to. If you need a more immediate way of lessening the voice of your gremlins as you work through this chapter, then try putting them in the freezer. Let me explain.

Since the gremlins truly believe they are keeping you safe, they *really* want to be heard. This means that if you ignore them, they can get sneaky and persistent in making sure their voices find you. (I liken this to a small child who is wanting to get your attention.) It therefore follows that you need to acknowledge them. For me, quietly acknowledging them in my head isn't enough. I need to allow their words to leave my head. Grab a piece of paper (or several sheets if you need them) and start writing down what your gremlins are telling you. Just keep writing. Don't filter it. Remember, they want to be heard. When you are done, and the gremlins are quiet, take the piece of paper and put it somewhere where it can't disturb you for the duration of the task you are working on. Think of this as placing your gremlins somewhere out of harm's way. Acknowledge to yourself that you are free to go back and collect it when you are ready.

Whenever that might be (maybe never). For me, since I work from home a lot, I find my freezer to be a good storage place for my gremlin's words. Now you are good to go. Let's start exploring your future.

In the garden of magical possibilities

I mentioned earlier that there are two broad approaches for envisioning your future. The first approach, outlined here, tends to be favoured by those people who have an 'intuition' preference. People who share this preference tend to live in the future and are immersed in the world of opportunities. They process information through patterns and impressions. They value inspiration and imagination.

> 'Intuition gives outlook and insight; it revels in the garden of magical possibilities as if they were real.'[23]
> — Carl Jung

That's where I want you to dream – in your own garden of magical possibilities. Future-oriented people with this preference for intuition can 'step out' of now and into the future, which enables them to perceive possibilities that are inherent in the present. If this sounds like you, then this activity should suit you well.

---

23 C J Jung, *The Psychology of Transference*, 1983, Routledge, London.

Step 1

Review your motivators as they are today. What's important to you? Start to consider how these motivators could be met in the future.

Step 2

Get yourself into an open, mindful head space. You want to be away from distractions. Meditation and breathing exercises are great ways to centre yourself for this exercise.

Step 3

Imagine yourself at a time in the future – this might be three to five years hence or at a landmark birthday or anniversary. Imagine what you want others to say about you. Spend some time in that future space. Recall what's important to you. What does 'good' look like? What talents do you want to come easily to you? Reflect on your motivators and how these are being met in this imagined future time. Give yourself permission to feel into this state. Remember to keep all your associations positive by imagining what *will* be rather than what *won't* be (ie don't think of the blue elephant).

Step 4

Now imagine a perfect day in the future, when you are living your heart's desire. Notice your surroundings. What type of environment are you in? What can you hear, taste, touch and smell? Who is with you? Paint yourself a vivid picture. Notice how you are feeling. What are the emotions of that now? Make it even more powerful by changing this picture into a movie.

Step 5

When you are ready, open your eyes and write an account of your perfect day. Just keep writing, capturing all the detail of what you saw, smelt, tasted, heard and felt. Then place this to one side.

Envisioning with a sensible awareness of reality

For those of you with a 'sensation' presence, you may prefer an approach where the starting point is the here and now. Jung described sensation as 'the sensible perception of reality'. By tuning in to what the five senses observe and building a concrete foundation that can be trusted, it is possible to step forward and imagine a future extrapolation of that reality.

Step 1

Start by reviewing the words you noted under the Current Reality exercise. Feel your awareness into these words as much as possible. Associate yourself and your five senses with what it is like to be you now.

Step 2

Either literally or figuratively, take a step forward. This represents you six months from now. What will you be doing? How will you be doing it? Why will you be doing it? Remember, this is from a place of growth so make sure your six-month vision takes account of this and is not just an image of you doing the same thing in six months.

Step 3

Now step forward another six months, to a year from today and ask yourself the same questions.

Step 4

Then repeat for two years from now, then four years from now (doubling up each time) until you choose to stop.

Step 5

Once you are finished, write a full account of what you see, smell, taste, hear and feel at this future point and place it to one side. You have now done the work necessary to move on.

Creating a vision of your 'what', 'how' and 'why bother'

Once you have completed one or both exercises you will be in a great place to answer the questions set out below. Grab yourself a fresh piece of flip chart paper and draw out the Performance Triangle as you did in the last chapter, or simply find a new space in your journal. Now we begin to journey into your future, and this time we are going to start with your 'why bother'.

Your 'why bother'

Continue to imagine yourself in this future point in time as you reflect on the following set of questions:

Consider yourself

- Why do you do what you do?
- What do you love doing?

- What gets you in flow?

- How supported do you feel in what you do?

- How challenged do you feel in what you do?

- How positive are you about making changes?

- How confident do you feel about what you do?

- What motivates you?

- What words describe how you feel about your work right now?

- How motivated are you?

Consider the team

Consider what teams you might be part of. Notice what impact working in these teams has on your 'why bother':

- What drives this team?

- When is this team most in flow?

- How supported do you feel in this team?

- How challenged do you feel in this team?

- How does this team handle change?

- How do you feel about being a member of this team?

- How does it serve you?

Consider the organisation

Consider what type of organisation you might be working in. Notice what impact this has on your 'why bother':

- What drives this organisation?

- What is its purpose?

- What are the key rewards and forms of recognition given that you most want?

- How does this organisation serve your needs?

Your 'how'

Now we are going to consider your 'how' at this future point in time. While answering these questions, be mindful of what is driving you and how this will impact on how you do what you do.

Consider yourself

- What are your new key skills?

- What are your new key talents?

- What extra 'life' experience do you have?

- What's your new key area of knowledge?

- What's your 'magic power'?

- What can people rely on you for?

- What behaviours come easy to you?

- How would you describe your style as a leader?

- How do others describe the way in which you work?

Consider your role in teams

Consider what teams you might be working within. What additional skills, behaviours, talents and/or knowledge will you be using in this team role that you haven't noted elsewhere?

- How do you contribute to the team's 'magic power'?

- How would you describe your style as a team member?

- What do other team members rely on you for in this role?

- Overall, what is the team's preferred way of working?

- What, if anything, is different about the way you show up in this team than when you are working elsewhere?

Consider the organisation you work for

- Consider which organisation your future self will be working in. What key skills does this type of organisation value?

- What talent does it attract and nurture?

- What's special about the way this business does what it does? How does this impact on how you do what you do?

- What key organisational cultural traits impact how you do what you do?

Your 'what'

Lastly, we want to explore your 'what'. This will be influenced by your 'why bother' (in terms of what is important to you) and your 'how'. Remember, we are still looking from the perspective of your future best version of yourself.

Consider yourself

- What does 'good' look like to you?

- What outcomes are you seeking?

- What have been your recent successes?

- What are you most proud of?

- Who do you regard as your peers?

- How do you describe what you do?

- What are the 'big ticket' items on your to-do list?

- What do you do for a living?

- What type of roles do you have? You might be a leader, a team member, an employee, a business owner, etc.

- What other roles do you have outside of work? You might be a parent, volunteer, sports team member, etc.

Consider the teams you work in

Now think more broadly about what role(s) you could have in teams in the future:

- What does this team exist for?

- What's your role in this team?

- What additional goals and/or objectives do you have as a result of being a member of this team?

- What have your recent biggest achievements in this team been?

- What are you most proud about having achieved by being a member of this team?

- How successful are you in this team?

Consider the organisation you work for

Now we turn to the type of organisation you imagine working in:

- What's the 'what' of the organisation? What does it do?

- Which part of that are you responsible for achieving?

- What role do you see this organisation having in society / the world at large?

- What are its key goals and objectives?

- What does it see as success?

- What are the biggest challenges facing the company right now? How does this impact you?

Allow yourself to reflect on your answers to these questions for a few days before you progress with the work in the following chapter.

Finding your North Star

The case below gives a real-life example of how one of my clients envisioned his future and the outcomes that resulted.

JULIAN: A CASE STUDY

When I first started working with Julian he was in a self-confessed rut. He'd been working in the same firm for a few years and was viewed as competent and, ultimately, a 'safe pair of hands'. He was helping his team land big value contracts but he kept finding himself doing the work behind the scenes rather than working directly with clients. His work was accurate. He delivered at a good pace. He was well liked within the team. To his boss, he appeared motivated. But Julian wanted more, so we worked on getting him more.

Having already explored how Julian saw himself (and how others saw him) in the present, using the Current Reality questions, we turned our attention to his future. Julian's work meant that he engaged his rational mind (rather than his creative mind) most of the time. He was more used to basing his world in the reality of now rather than using his gut to imagine different ways of working. He couldn't see where his future was taking him.

After explaining the two methods for envisioning, Julian chose the intuitive method. He wanted to be free of the reality in which he found himself and free of the gremlins which he knew would be waiting to ask him, 'How are you going to do that, then?' at every turn. He was willing to give it a go and he was willing to play with some ideas.

I guided him through the exercise in a large room where he was safely able to close his eyes, centre himself and literally step into his future vision. I encouraged him to think about all aspects of his future best life: who he would be spending time with; how work felt; how his motivators were being met in all aspects of life and work. I didn't want him to think in specifics; I wanted him to stay in the abstract with his emotions.

He didn't share his whole vision with me at that point. It was for him to know. I was simply there during the subsequent coaching sessions to ensure that he mastered the skills, behaviours and mindset he knew he would need to become that person he had so clearly seen in his future.

A couple of years later, he was keen to give me an update and we met for a coffee. Not only had he succeeded in being appointed a partner in the firm he was working with, another part of his dream had come true: he was about to get married and they were expecting a baby. These were all things he had envisioned and had no idea how he was going to bring them about. He explained to me that his vision was so clear that it had become his guiding light, his North Star.

Wishful thinking or neuroscience in action?

By setting out what he wanted to have happen, Julian gave his mind a focus. In the deafening cacophony of stimuli that your brain filters every second of every day, providing your mind with a focus enables it to look out for those pieces of data that help you, allowing you to ignore those which do not. It is our brain's Reticular Activating System (RAS) which enables us to do this. By setting out our intentions and goals, the RAS is triggered. It highlights opportunities we might have otherwise missed. Let me demonstrate with a simple experiment. In a moment, I would like you to close your eyes and think of your favourite colour. I would like you to turn up the intensity of that colour so that it fills your mind's eye completely. Go ahead and spend thirty seconds imagining that colour. Then read on.

Now, with your eyes open, look around and notice how many things are in your line of sight which are that colour. If you have imagined the colour well enough, you'll find items 'popping' out at you. Chances are you didn't even notice them before. Now they seem to stand out from the rest. That's your RAS in action. Can you see how imagining your future through all your senses can enable you to focus in on and sense all the occurrences that could lead to that future? Add this to the fact that in asking the questions in this chapter you are creating neural pathways which will lead to new discoveries, and suddenly that super-computer is working super hard to bring your future self into creation.

Summary

- Envisioning the future is about dreaming beyond the now.

- You can use an intuition-based approach, a sensing-based approach, or both.

- Your future self is being impacted by the teams and organisations in which you serve.

- To dream big, you need to let go of your gremlins.

- By being clear in your vision, you trigger your Reticular Activating System to seek out opportunities that help make your dream a reality.

SIX

creAte: Align

'Only when your intention and actions are in alignment can you create the reality you desire.'[24]
— Steve Maraboli

When working with organisations, the same theme comes up time and time again: a lack of alignment. At an organisational level, I see the parallel tracks carved by team members working with a silo mentality. Within teams, I see footprints in the sand that tell more of a 'give and take' story, a tennis match, a contest, rather than members of a team working together. Individuals are left to see, hear and feel the internal struggle of 'toeing the line' rather than being true to themselves. With so much out of alignment,

---

24 Steve Maraboli, *Life, the Truth, and Being Free*, 2009, A Better Today Publishing, New York.

it is hardly a surprise that the results organisations achieve are hard won. Like a person with their joints out of place, they struggle to walk, but struggle they must, wishing it was easier and wondering why it is all so hard.

When a team gains alignment, I liken it to the relief you get from a visit to the chiropractor. Something clicks and there is a sudden shift in movement and mood. The team can access 'flow' and works as a single unit. Have you ever experienced that magical moment when a team is working together, working as one? As with our physical aches and pains, we need to deliberately stay in alignment. All too often, teams slip back into their old ways of working. Ingrained habits mix with the environment and culture and bring back the old, familiar niggles. And because of their familiarity, the symptoms are not alarming enough to attract attention at first (think of the 'boiling frog' experiment). It's only when the pain gets too much that an 'away day' is planned, with a facilitator acting as a metaphorical chiropractor, and work starts on realignment again. What if you could avoid this? What if there was a regular practice (a habit) you could use to stay in alignment?

So often I see teams who have the ingredients for success. They have the 'what' (a clear strategy), the 'how' (skills and behaviours) and the 'why bother' (motivation) but they don't have the recipe. How do you blend the ingredients that are key: how do you align them? This chapter will show you how.

What is alignment?

Organisations have talked about alignment for years; about the 'golden thread' that aligns each person's objectives to the organisational goals. They may say their personal development plans have 'a line of sight' to the 'what' which the organisation needs, but often they fail to recognise the need for alignment to motivation.

To further understand why alignment is so important, let's delve further into what it means: The first definition of alignment is about things being arranged 'in a straight line or correct relative positions'. This definition, then, is about ordering and designing appropriately, having 'geographical' alignment. The second definition is about 'a position of agreement or alliance' and includes synonyms like 'union', 'partnership', 'affiliation' and 'coalition'. It implies that if you are to get anything done, it would seem sensible (and probably essential) to agree with the other party – to be in coalition.

What happens when there is lack of alignment?

Let me give you common examples of what lack of alignment looks like when I first start working with clients:

At an organisational level, I hear about sales teams being hugely successful in selling product but leaving operations teams unable to fulfil the orders. I hear blame bubbling up pointing to the elusive 'they' ('If only *they* had told us about their plans…', '*They* don't understand how much pressure we are under…' or '*They* haven't done what they said they would…'). With everyone pointing the finger at everyone else, I start to wonder who 'they' are?

At team level, I see some people really struggling with their workload, while others in the same team fail to support them, instead believing that it is the struggler's problem. I see people working by themselves forgetting to bring others with them. And I see resentment growing and frustrations building as people behave in ways which just don't seem to make sense.

At an individual level, I see people whose bodies are being put under tremendous strain to the point of burnout and yet they plough on, believing that if they dig deep enough, they will deliver what is expected of them and recover later. If this is you, do you truly make the space for this recovery? For what? And what is the cost to your physical and mental health for riding this rollercoaster of boom and almost bust?

The solution lies in achieving alignment with motivation. In case you need convincing, go back to the examples you came up with in Chapter 2 when you thought about times when you were least motivated and most motivated. What impact did your lack of motivation have on your skills level, your behaviour and the results you achieved?

Gaining alignment

In the preceding chapters, you have done the foundational work. Now you can start to gain alignment. There are two areas of alignment to focus on. The first is the internal alignment between your 'what', 'how' and 'why bother'. The second is alignment between your 'what' with the 'what' of your team and organisation; alignment between your 'how' with the 'how' of your team and organisation and finally (and perhaps most importantly), alignment between your 'why bother' and the 'why bother' of your team and your organisation. This is external alignment, and this builds a coalition between you and others.

Internal alignment

When you are aligned internally, what you do and how you do it happens with ease. When you are out of alignment, what you do and how you do it happens with dis-ease. What we are looking for here, and want to bring conscious awareness to, is how your 'whats', 'hows' and 'why bothers' link to each other.

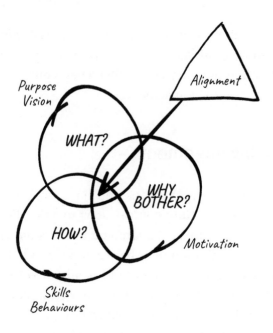

Alignment

Go back and look at your Current Reality work. Use a highlighter to pick out the key words. What links can you see between your 'what', 'how' and 'why bother'? Are they in alignment? If they are, and you are getting the outcomes you are seeking, you are in a good place on which to build your future. If they are out of kilter, look to see how you can make some changes to bring them into alignment. If they are small changes, chances are you can go ahead and make them now. If they are big changes, note them down and look at them again when we look at turning your plans into action in the following two chapters.

Now, have a look at your Envision work. Again, use a highlighter to pick out key words. What links can you see between your 'why bother', 'how' and 'what'? How aligned are they? If your 'what' does not align to your 'why bother', go back and re-imagine how they could align. For example, if your 'what' is about being a self-employed consultant and your 'why bother' is motivated by security, then maybe you could have more security by being an employed consultant. If your 'how' does not align to your 'why bother', go back and re-work this. The point is you need to think differently if you want to create a future that is different. You don't need precise answers to your 'what' questions – just a sense of what could be. This is where really knowing your motivators starts to pay dividends. Talking through your dreams with a third party, a coach, can help unblock further limiting beliefs and remove any blinkered vision. As you start working from your 'why bother', you will find your 'how' and 'what' will emerge naturally. Trust the process – it works.

Tasks you don't enjoy doing

I'm not one to dwell on negatives, but it helps with alignment if you consider the things you *don't* enjoy doing. You may have discounted a whole role or opportunity because of aspects of how it is currently done. For example, part of your imagined role might involve writing reports, something which you simply don't enjoy. Ask yourself what it is about writing reports that you don't like. What would need to happen to make it more enjoyable? Think about the different ways in which you could write those reports. Maybe brainstorming ideas with someone before you write the report would be more energising, or taking yourself off to an environment you enjoy writing in would make it more engaging. Maybe it's about realising what completing the report will enable. For example, if you are motivated by making a difference, what more of a difference will you make by being the author of that report? (If you can see no impact, do question why it is needed. So often organisations ask for papers and reports because 'that's what we have always done' or you have managers who like reports simply because it gives them reassurance. Consider other ways you could give people what they are looking for, for example, through a presentation or a Q&A session, etc.)

External alignment

External alignment is about how you connect your 'what', 'how' and 'why bother' to that of the team(s) and organisation you work with. It's about making sure that 'what' you do aligns to 'what' the team and organisation is charged with delivering, that your 'how' (your skills and behaviours) aligns to the 'how' of the team and organisation and about aligning your 'why bother' to the 'why bother' of the team and the organisation. When you start sharing what you are enthused to do, it's surprising how teams and organisations make space for that to become a reality.

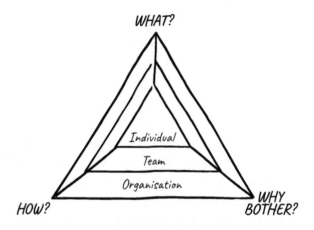

WHAT?

Individual

Team

Organisation

HOW?

WHY BOTHER?

Alignment to the team and the organisation

When your 'what' is aligned to the team and organisation, you are all going in the same direction: you're all following the same North Star. There is efficiency in this – all effort is focused on specific outcomes. No effort is wasted on things that might suit an individual, but don't contribute to the bigger picture. There is an effectiveness in this – everything you and the teams do is chosen deliberately to bring about the desired results.

When your 'how' is aligned to the team, and the team's 'how' is aligned to yours, you willingly and readily choose to use certain behaviours and skills that complement the team. Synergy is created. When your 'how' is aligned on a greater scale with other people in the organisation then this influences culture, for culture is simply an expression of 'how things are done around here'.

When your 'why bother' is aligned to the team, you have a reason for behaving as you do. You can see 'what's in it for you'. You will experience rewards that meet your motivators and encourage you to keep going as part of the team. You will feel authentic. For example, if you are motivated by creativity and innovation, you might uncover a greater sense of this by working more within the team and the results will drive you to do it more. You might discover the sense of expertise you feel when working with others and being able to share and/or build your knowledge, so you choose to work with the team more. You will find opportunities for your unique talents to shine within a team. You'll even be willing to push through some behaviours you don't like (perhaps such as having to turn up to meetings at inconvenient times) so that you can experience the rewards you value.

When you align your 'why bother' to the organisation's, you will experience an even greater sense of congruence. You will know *why* you are working for this organisation at this time. You will feel engaged with the organisation. When fully aligned, you will place real value on the rewards and opportunities the organisation provides you as they meet your motivators. For example, if you value freedom, actively choose to focus on opportunities for flexi-working. Employee benefits such as pension and healthcare are valued by those seeking security. Chill-out areas designed to encourage those serendipitous moments where you bump into the right person at the right time and create new ideas and opportunities are welcomed by those driven by creativity and variety.

Now is a good time to go back and look at your Current Reality notes and identify how much alignment you currently have between yourself, the team(s) you work in and the organisation. Is there anything you need to do now to build greater alignment before moving forward or does what you have explored in your Envisioned future already move you towards this? Look at your Envisioned future and ensure there is solid alignment between you, your team and your organisation.

Alignment in teams is not 'groupthink'

So, why is alignment so important in teams?

Firstly, it is important to clarify that alignment does not equate to 'groupthink'. Groupthink is a phenomenon which occurs when a group of well-intentioned people make irrational or poor decisions, driven by the desire to conform, avoid dissent and prioritise harmony in the group. When team members are aligned, they agree with team priorities and understand the reasoning behind them. They can see why they need to complete things in a particular manner. When individual frustrations arise (which they are bound to do), they can see past the behaviour to the reasons for that behaviour. When people are congruent, and aligned to the ultimate outcome, they will find solutions to make sure they get there, but this does not result in 'groupthink' – and nor should it.

In his best-selling book *The Five Dysfunctions of a Team*, Patrick Lencioni identified that one of the five key elements essential to team success is commitment. He found that only by team members being able to put all their ideas on the table were they able to commit to outcomes.[25] Commitment is therefore rightfully preceded by debate, and often conflict and disagreement. This sharing of ideas aids alignment: having the opportunity to articulate not only your idea, but also why it is important to you, the team and the organisation, allows healthy conflict within a context of wider agreement. All of this is preceded by trust. A deeper understanding of why each person does what they do helps build a stronger foundation of trust. Sharing our 'why bothers' brings about greater vulnerability in the team – a vital component of trust.

---

25 Patrick Lencioni, *The Five Dysfunctions of a Team*, 2002, John Wiley and Sons, New York.

Alignment is the right path, not necessarily the easy path

As with 'flow', just because alignment creates a feeling of effortlessness, it's not a sign to say you have taken the easy path. If you are truly living in alignment with your motivators, truly committed to showing up as the best version of yourself, then this will have taken hard work. The difference is that by being in alignment, you create energy while being out of alignment uses it up. With alignment, even in your darkest moments you will know why you are doing what you are doing; you will know you are on the right path (your 'what') and using the right skills (your 'how') fuelled by the right motivators (your 'why bother').

I'm OK but the system is not

It is entirely possible that there is lack of alignment at a macro level between what the organisation is seeking and what a division, directorate, region or team is being charged with delivering. It is also possible that the skills and behaviours an organisation says it wants to develop are not the ones which get role modelled, encouraged or rewarded. Finally, it is probable that the organisation does not communicate its 'why' in any meaningful terms or that this message gets drowned out by key performance indicators, targets and numbers. These macro levels of misalignment are not the focus of this book but I see this in so many organisations that it would be remiss of me to not offer some words of advice. Should you be experiencing this level of lack of alignment, the remainder of this chapter is for you.

You don't need to wait for others to act first

Years ago, I was working with an organisation that said it wanted to introduce better appraisals and performance management. It was in the days when 'specific, measurable, achievable, relevant and time-bound' (SMART) objectives were all the rage. This business was struggling with performance at all levels – individual, team and organisation. I was charged with designing and implementing a new appraisal system. I was told the senior management were on board with this but when I started rolling out the programme and running training sessions on how to use it, I was met with resistance. Managers felt they were unable to set objectives for their teams when they had not had their own objectives set by senior management. Knowing the senior management as I did, I knew that they were unlikely to get around to setting any. It was a classic case of 'do what I say and not as I do'. Even then, at the start of my career, I had a deep sense of leading from self. As Gandhi said, 'Be the change you want to see in the world.' That was the advice I gave those managers. Sure enough, those managers who could align their own desire (motivation) to build better performance in their teams did not wait for instructions from on high about objectives. They knew what needed to be done. Nor did they need clarification on the how. It was these middle managers who changed the way this company performed. They led where others, more senior to them, failed to do so.

Use your personal power

I presume that you are reading this book because you are seeking a better way to lead, manage and enable your team. Given my definition of leadership, I don't believe you need a position of authority (the title of 'leader') to do this. You have personal power irrespective of your title. This personal power comes from channelling your energy and your core behaviours towards an outcome you are seeking. If you are seeking to influence the need for greater alignment in your business then work out how you will do this and make sure it's being fuelled by your motivators. It's easy to stand on the side-lines moaning. Become part of the success story by taking initiative responsibly.

Get help

My hope is that this book will clarify what you can do to enable the best version of yourself. With practice, the tools in this book will set you in the right direction, but the change many of you are seeking in the organisations you work with will have to be a collaborative effort. You cannot do this alone. Yes, you can role model the changes. Yes, you can influence the changes. Making all the necessary changes will also require the energy and talents of others and that's where you need to ask for help. This might come from like-minded people within your team. It might come from your People and Organisational Development teams. It might come from an external organisation like mine. The important thing is you ask for help – help to deliver something bigger than yourself. More about this when we look at Engagement in Chapter 9.

Summary

- Without alignment, efforts are wasted, forced, and can be downright painful.

- There are two types of alignment:
    - Internal alignment between your 'what', 'how' and 'why bother'.

    - External alignment between your 'what', 'how' and 'why bother' and that of the teams and organisations in which you serve.

- There are steps you can take to gain alignment even if the rest of the organisation isn't there yet. It starts with you.

- Ask for help and collaborate. You can't do this alone, nor should you.

creaTe: Test-out

By now, you should see the gap between where you are now and where you want to be. Hopefully you can sense the alignment between your 'what', 'how' and 'why bother' so you feel fired up to take action to enable the future, expanded version of yourself. You should see the (growing) alignment between you, your team(s) and your organisation and have a sense of the changes you want to make to strengthen this further. Before you action these changes, there are two final steps in the CREATE model.

Why you need to 'Test-out'

So far, the work you have done is mainly in your head. You have grounded yourself in your Current Reality, imagined your future and addressed Alignment. That process by itself creates motivation. I hope you can sense that.

The 'Test-out' stage of the CREATE model is about considering all possible and probable twists and turns of the journey on which you are about to embark, testing out ways of minimising problems and maximising opportunities. This provides you with extra motivation by telling your brain you are ready for this, no matter what comes up.

'Test-out' is like looking at the weather before you begin a car journey to make sure you are prepared – windscreen wash full, de-icer at the ready and snow-chains packed. It's like tuning into the traffic report to see what diversions there might be along the way. Don't just plan for the worst though – if the weather forecast is great, think about how taking the scenic route might enhance your journey.

This step ensures you are prepared ahead of time, so you are able to make the most of any unplanned opportunities along the way and not be derailed by potential issues along the way. It helps provide greater motivation.

There are two categories to look at when Testing-out: internal and external. Internal tests are those to do with mindset, psychology and motivation. External tests are more to do with other people, availability of resources and the changing world in which we live. To use an analogy: Imagine you are about to embark on a car journey. The destination is clear but the route will take you through places you have never been before. As you set out on your journey, all is well. You settle into your familiar routine and get so engrossed in your audiobook that you are driving on 'autopilot', occasionally re-surfacing at traffic lights or when someone cuts in front of you. All is going well. The journey is proceeding as you thought it would.

Then, after a couple of hours of driving, things change. Your satnav directs you into a traffic jam. It's obvious it has been there for a while. You can see the next exit isn't for miles. You crawl along at a snail's pace, teased by the road signs warning you not to go above 30 mph (chance would be a fine thing, you're barely into double figures). As minutes turn into an hour, you check and recheck the fuel gauge, worrying you won't have enough fuel to get you to the next exit. To cap it all, you desperately need a 'call of nature'. One hour turns into two. You are now bored, worried, frustrated and about to burst. You start telling yourself things like, 'You should have planned this better, you always hit traffic jams, this is why you usually go by train...' You completely lose interest in the reason you were travelling in the first place and can't see the point in going on with the journey. Your day has been ruined. Then you notice the traffic start to move. Whatever was causing the delay has cleared and you start your journey again without a hitch, but your mood is stuck and it's still been a painful journey.

If you were to plot your physical journey, it would appear much like the one you had planned: same route, it just took longer. If you were to plot your *emotional* journey (ie what was going through your mind), it would be very different to what you had planned. If you had been able to, you would have likely given up and turned around. The skills you needed on the journey were different to what you had imagined you'd need. Resilience, patience and positivity might have served you better than self-defeat, frustration and negativity. If only you'd had the foresight to anticipate any problems you might have encountered along the way to have been better prepared. If only you had 'tested out'. It is much the same with your personal journey ahead.

Avoiding obstacles and embracing opportunities

To avoid or minimise obstacles and embrace opportunities, it is worth imagining the journey you are about to go on. Go back to the words you noted for your Envisioned future. Feel them once again. Imagine you are in that future place in glorious Technicolor and Dolby surround sound. Feel the emotions and take your time being there. See it, smell it, taste it, touch it and hear it.

Now step back in time. If you were envisioning five years from now, step back to three years from now. Connect into what needs to be happening at that point in time to enable the future you have just seen. What is different? What is the same? When you are clear, step back eighteen months from now and do the same thing. Then nine months, four months, two months, one month from now. Each time, feeling into the emotions. Remember to think about 'what' you will be doing, 'how' you will be doing it, and connecting into the energy of 'why' you are doing it. Finally, bring this vision to two weeks from now.

When you are ready, ask yourself, 'What are the obstacles that could get in the way of this envisioned future?' Keep writing down your answers and if you get stuck, ask the question again to see if more comes up. Go through at least two 'stuck-points' to drain yourself of ideas. Rephrase the question if it helps: change it to, 'What could stop me succeeding?' Write everything down that comes to mind – no self-editing at this stage. Staying with your Envisioned future, ask yourself, 'What opportunities are open to me?' Continue writing everything that comes to mind and going through two 'stuck-points'. Then ask, 'What possibilities await me?'

The next step is to check your answers. From your obstacles list, see which ones might be just your gremlins talking: obstacles based on self-limiting beliefs and not facts. What would enable you to turn these beliefs around? Maybe you have some of the answers on your opportunities list? Then review the remaining obstacles on your list. They are likely to be about external events or resources. Spend time identifying what would need to happen to overcome these. You will likely have answers to most of them now or know you will be able to figure them out. Again, your opportunities list might help you here.

Finally, review your opportunities list. Is there anything you want to change about your Envisioned future given what you realise is possible and available to you? What could you make space for? If you need to, re-imagine your future and the steps back to now.

Looking in the rear-view mirror

When you drive, you don't spend all your time looking forward through the windscreen. You also look at your mirrors to see what's happening behind you and determine how to react. Do you need to slow down, not overtake, perhaps speed up? When someone is driving close to your bumper you will drive differently to when the road is clear behind you. When the weather is appalling you hold your space on the road in a different way, taking extra account of what is behind you and can literally crash into you. This is a useful metaphor for how to step into your future: it requires you to take account of your past and how it impacts on you – both positively and negatively.

Also take account of events to your side and how they could catch you off guard or offer a new route forward. Awareness brings clarity, and clarity brings choice. I am not suggesting you look every few seconds (since you aren't travelling at 70 mph) but I am suggesting you look carefully before signalling your intent and then moving forward.

Take a good look in the rear-view mirror of your mind now by looking back at any notes you made on the inverted Performance Triangle. (We covered this when looking at your Current Reality in Chapter 4.) Look at the undesirable results you have brought about (the 'what'), the unhelpful behaviours that led you there ('how') and what was driving this ('why bother'). These are potential obstacles and need to be addressed now, before you set off on your new journey. They might be fuelled by gremlins, but you know what to do with them. They might be old habits or behaviours that no longer serve you well. If so, be explicit about the new behaviours you *do* want to exhibit and work out what's in it for you (your 'why bother'). As you move forward, acknowledge and celebrate when you get it right. This will provide your brain with new reference points and make it easier for you to build a new habit. If you fall short, learn from it and revisit what drove these actions. If a lack of clarity about your direction was the problem, make sure you have 20/20 vision this time.

Then look at your Current Reality notes. What resources will you take forward with you? What outcomes will you build on? What behaviours will hold you in good stead? What motivations will drive you forward positively? Having this awareness will help propel you forwards with more certainty and provide you with sturdy foundations on which to build.

Saying 'no' more

To make sure you bring about your Envisioned future, you will likely have to start saying 'no' to certain tasks and people. Some of the things you used to do, the tasks you performed, no longer fit with the next part of your journey. Take a moment to think about what and who you might need to say 'no' to.

Having your Envisioned future will help you separate the work you do need to do (your 'big rocks') from those you no longer need to do (your distractions). 'Big rocks' are your areas of focus that support your future vision. Having certainty about your 'rocks' and using them to guide conscious choices about the steps you are taking to bring your future into existence is a new habit that will serve you well. (Dr Stephen R. Covey uses this term in his approach to life and time management.[26])

---

26 Dr Stephen R. Covey, 'Big Rocks', not dated, www.youtube.com/ watch?v=zV3gMTOEWt8 [accessed 13 February 2020].

A straight 'no' often causes offence, so you will need to apply some skill and judgement here. There are also some pre-emptive steps to prevent people asking you in the first place (more about this in the next chapter). When people do ask you to perform tasks that no longer form part of your future, engage with them and ask them what they are looking for. Help them explore whether the task still needs to be done. If it does, help them find a more suitable person to do it.

Small changes today have a big impact on tomorrow

When faced with the big vision you have for yourself, it can seem like a large mountain to climb. Remember that simply choosing to make one or two simple changes in the way you operate will have a compound impact on where you end up. A slight two degree shift today will lead you to a different place tomorrow.

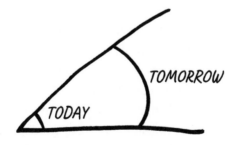

Small changes today have a big impact on tomorrow

Be careful who you surround yourself with

Look around at the people you work with. Who do you pay most attention to? Who do you take your lead from? If they are people that nourish your dreams and inspire you then carry on. If they are people who fill you with doubt and feed your gremlins, immediately remove them from your circle of influencers. Make a conscious decision to no longer listen to them when it comes to your future.

You are that person, today

A lot of people live their life saying something along the lines of, 'When I have x, then I'll be able to do y and then I'll be z.' For example: 'When I have the next promotion, then I will be able to delegate more and then I will be less stressed.'

This 'have', 'do', 'be' piece is surely the wrong way around. If you look at most of what you are envisioning for yourself, are you not that person now? In the example above, you can take immediate action to be less stressed which may or may not involve delegating and certainly doesn't require a promotion. If we live our lives thinking we need to 'have' in order to 'do' so we can 'be' something, we are missing the point. You have so much of what you need to deliver on your future *now*. Much of it is about mindset and choosing to operate from that place. You are that person today – you just don't realise it yet.

Summary

- Before you pursue your dreams, check you are all set for the journey. Knowing in advance that you have what you need to overcome bumps in the road means they will be more easily overcome or avoided altogether.

- Check out hidden opportunities. By looking ahead, you might see some possibilities you didn't see before. Seize them.

- Look in your rear-view mirrors to adjust your plans. Bringing awareness to your past adds greater certainty to how you will drive forwards.

- Small shifts today will make a big difference tomorrow.

- Remember: Be, Do, Have. You are that person today.

EIGHT

creatE: Engage

W e are social beings. We need others to support us, challenge us, guide us and protect us. I believe we can only discover our true potential by working with others. If you think of the people you most admire, do they achieve what they do by themselves, or indeed, for themselves?

This stage of the CREATE model is about Engaging with others so that you can stay aligned and stay on track. It marks the start of putting your ideas into action.

Big rocks

As you look at your Envisioned future, it might be tempting to spend hours planning each step like you would a major project. This might be helpful, but in my experience, changing behaviour doesn't take much notice of a 'project plan'. As human beings we can be unpredictable and so we need to work more flexibly than plans sometimes allow. We need a way of moving forward that can be sped up or slowed down depending on how energised we feel and what results we are achieving.

We also need a method which doesn't trigger the competitive, single focused ways of doing things which so many traditional ways of planning encourage. In my experience, being target and output driven is counterproductive as all too often people start competing rather than recognising that they are on the same team. We need an approach which is outcome driven: an approach which aligns 'what', 'how' and 'why bother'.

Start by identifying your 'big rocks'. These are driven by your motivators and aligned to your 'what'. They can usually be summarised into just a few words (which makes them memorable). Less is more here – aim to have one, two or three rocks. If you struggle with this, chances are you are too much in the detail and you need to chunk them up.

The next step is something which I encourage you to make a weekly habit. Connect back to both your Envisioned future and your 'big rocks' and ask yourself what actions you can take this week which will enable that future. What will be different by this time next week? Check in on the skills and behaviours you need to take these actions and double check how they align to your 'how'. And, of course, make sure they align to your 'why bother' for it is this which will give you the energy to succeed. Take a step back and review your progress every month or so to pick up what's working and what's not so you can adjust your pace.

You many need to loosen your grip on the timeframe associated with your Envisioned future. The more you prioritise meeting goals for the sake of it, the more you will take on that narrow focus again. A narrow focus, by definition, is one which does not look laterally and so is less creative, By using a narrow focus, you are more likely to fall short. It is also one which starves you of the human 'experience' of savouring the senses as you go about your daily work. Trust that by having weekly and monthly check-ins, you will make timely progress.

Set out your stall

It is highly unlikely that you will be able to achieve what you want from your future without engaging with others. I'd even go so far as to say it is impossible. Chances are some of the people who will accompany you on the next stage of your growth have been with you for a while. They will be used to your normal patterns of behaviour, so as much as you needed to become vividly aware of your Current Reality, so might they. They might be carrying around an old 'version' of you and might, unknowingly, be reinforcing it through their asks, actions and feedback.

If they are to stay on the journey with you, it will be useful to tell them where you are heading. They need to know your 'what'. What is important to you now, and in the future? What does 'good' look like to you now, and how does it change in the future? They also need to know your 'how'. What skills and behaviours are you nurturing and building to carry you on your journey, and what skills are you putting into retirement? What experiences and knowledge will you be deliberately courting? As some of this information might be news to them, they will also want to know your 'why bother'. Why are you wanting to go in this direction and why are you wanting to prioritise these skills and behaviours? Giving them this insight will mean you are sharing with them what is driving you now. It will give them a window in your world. I call this sharing of your 'what', 'how' and 'why bother' *setting out your stall*. You are setting out your intentions, your determination and your motivation. It enables people to have a clear, sharply focused picture of you and what you are about, rather than their current, perhaps rather fuzzy one. By doing this you make it easier for others to decide how they want to work with you. They know what you are, and what you are not.

By sharing your aspirations, you can encourage others to do the same. Imagine if everyone in your team had as clear a picture of their own future as you now do. If they did, you could build alignment where your ideas overlap with theirs. You can make some conscious choices about what to do if there is a gap between what you want and what they want. You know where you each stand and you can work together deliberately on that which is shared.

The importance of sharing motivation

It is almost impossible to guess what motivates someone: it's so tempting to make assumptions based on behaviours but often these are woefully misleading. If you worked in a bar, you wouldn't wait for colleagues to find out about your peanut allergy – you'd offer that information up-front, so people understood why you weren't willing to top up the bar snacks. Sharing your motivators with peers helps to build trust, which in turn helps us engage in healthy conflict and decision-making.

By initiating conversations with your peers about motivation, you will also be leading the way for more open and real conversations about who we are and why we work as we do. By making this often-hidden aspect of your 'self' more visible, and by building language around it, people will more readily take responsibility for their own motivation. Hearing *you* talk about motivation gives permission for others to do the same. When your colleagues understand why you prioritise the things you do and why you may fail to work in ways which make sense to them, you will be better placed to have your motivators met on a regular basis. This will keep you energised at work, and your energy will be contagious.

Catching people doing it right

A big advantage of setting out your stall is that you build accountability. By sharing what you are and what you want to become, you can more easily invite people to give you feedback. They now know what 'good' looks like and so will be able to give you feedback when you veer off course. You want them to catch you doing this early so you can make the small corrections needed to get back on track. Be sure to explicitly ask for feedback of this nature.

What is of vital importance, and often overlooked, is feedback that you are on-course. Sometimes when we try out a new approach or a new behaviour (including prioritising certain courses of action) it can make so much sense to others that our actions go under the radar. We might be taking a big risk in behaving in this new way and yet no one seems to be noticing. Some people might be happy receiving no recognition for their efforts as they will consider that 'no news is good news' but how much more energised would they feel, how much more able to continue to grow, if they did receive positive reinforcement via feedback. This act of 'catching people doing it right' was first popularised by the leadership guru Ken Blanchard.[27] In an age where we are so used to either being ignored or being criticised, his simple approach has much to offer. As part of setting out your stall, share the importance of this way of working and ask for regular feedback of this nature – and be prepared to do the same for others. It's a remarkably effective way of emphasising new behaviours and building habits.

Setting intentions

There is much evidence to suggest that when we set out our intentions before embarking on a task, we achieve more. Stating intention helps the brain (the RAS) sort through millions of bits of data into that which we need to pay attention to, and that which we can discard. To set your intention, you must be deliberate. To be deliberate you must be present. A great way of setting clear intentions to is be clear about what you want to 'think', 'do' and 'know' through the actions you are taking.

Becoming conscious – the deliberate you

In a culture where 'busyness' is rewarded, it can be easy to fall back into old patterns and old ways of

---

27 Ken Blanchard, 'Catch People Doing Something Right', not dated, www.kenblanchardbooks.com/catch-people-doing-something-right [accessed 13 February 2020]

thinking. My desire for you is to become more deliberate, more awake. We are so used to thinking about what we have just done and what we are about to do that we often fail to be in the present. It is through having presence that we get our best ideas, are most connected, lose the deafening sound of our unhelpful gremlins and are simply more of who we are. Only from here can we access our full potential. It is here that we access our flow.

For many of us, our modus operandi is 'do, do, do', yet to be present we need to 'be, be, be'. You might feel you need some help to get into your 'being state'. That's where the practice of mindfulness comes in. For some of you, the idea of stopping 'doing' in order to 'be' will sound pointless, a waste of time, and you might catch yourself thinking, 'How will doing less, allow me to achieve more?' I ask you to simply try it. Is running around, with never a moment to draw breath, really how you want to spend tomorrow, next week, next year or more?

Being present: an example

I was facilitating an 'away day' with a hard-working group of facilitators some years ago and they wanted to get to know each other better. The exercise I asked them to do was an easy one: to share with everyone in the room what a typical working day was like for them. The aim was for people to appreciate what pressures each of them were under (both in and outside of work) so they could better understand why colleagues behaved the way they did and build empathy and compassion. This was a high achieving group who were ambitious about what the team could achieve. There was a lot of excitement in the room. A real sense of energy. I noticed that one person in the room had a different energy. She sat almost glowing, hardly moving. Calm and all-knowing, not in an egotistical way, simply an 'at-oneness' type of way. As I think of her now, I can almost see the radiance surrounding her. In my extroverted state it was almost disturbing, and her presence had a profound impact on me.

We went around the room as people shared accounts of their typical day. There was a group of women who got up super early in the morning, completed chores, had long commutes and arrived at their desks between 8.30am and 9am feeling they had already done a day's work. There were others who scrambled out of bed at the last moment and rushed to work every day. And then there was my radiant friend. She told us how she woke and did her meditation practice for thirty minutes or so every day, without fail, before making her way to work. She had children and she had a long commute, yet she arrived at work ready, deliberate, calm and relaxed. She was a high performer and well respected. She had simply chosen a different way of being.

Be mindful

To experience some of this radiance for yourself, try the following exercise. Read the instructions through first so you can prepare a suitable space; somewhere you can safely close your eyes.

Ground yourself by paying attention to that part of your body which is closest to the ground – it may be your feet if you are standing, through the chair if you are sitting, or it may be your whole body if you are lying down. Imagine roots growing out of that part of your body, roots that at burrowing out into the earth below, steadying you. Stay with this until you feel connected to the floor. Once you feel grounded, imagine a bright light above your head pulling your consciousness up to the sky and beyond.

Slowly breathe in through your nose for a count of four. Hold your breath for the count of four. Then release, through your mouth, for a count four. Repeat this for a couple of minutes – focusing purely on the movement of your breath. When other thoughts creep in (which they will), notice them but try and let them drift away into the light rather than holding on to them.

If you begin to feel light-headed, shorten your in-breath and lengthen your out-breath to rebalance your O_2/CO_2 levels. Now allow your breath to return to its natural flow. Nothing to correct. Nothing to change. Just notice it.

When you are ready, slowly open your eyes, allowing yourself to adjust to the light and then wiggle your toes and fingers to bring energy back into your body.

Practice this regularly – ideally two or three times a day and notice how much calmer, connected and present you feel. It seems counter-intuitive to pause like this in a busy day but it' in the space you create while in this present state that your mind settles and recharges so you can begin again from a greater place of awareness. It's powerful stuff.

Summary

- Set yourself up for success – engage with others. You can't up-level by yourself.

- 'Set out your stall' to others so you can see where you have alignment and where you don't.

- Encourage and give feedback. Catch people doing it right.

- Become conscious, become deliberate.

- Plan your progress in a more human 'being' centred way than human 'doing' centred way. You are not a project to be managed.

- Practice mindfulness daily.

- Set weekly intentions.

NINE

Learn And Embed

The focus of this book is to help you CREATE the space to step into *your* version of leadership and the space for you to grow into your expanded self. This chapter will explore how you can bridge the gap between where you are now and where you want to be in terms of your 'how' through learning, and how to embed what you learn.

You should have a good sense of what skills, behaviours and experiences you want to develop by now. Some will be new to you. Some will be extensions of what you already have. How will you obtain these skills, gain this experience and develop these behaviours? There are a multitude of options available to you.

70:20:10

Some years ago, evidence emerged to suggest that around 70% of learning comes from experience (on the job), around 20% comes from social learning with colleagues and just 10% comes through formal learning such as classroom training or online courses. While this model isn't intended to be prescriptive, it certainly sits well with my philosophy that learning is a self-directed activity available within the every day.

In the last few years alone, learning has become much easier to access via self-service whether it be formal online academies provided through work, online membership packages or simply navigating your way through TED talks, YouTube and Google. With so much content available, we need to know how you transfer this theory into action; how you will land the learning.

Doer or thinker?

When it comes to learning are you a 'doer' (a person who prefers to act before reflecting on their experience) or a 'thinker' (a person who prefers to think through concepts before taking action)? There are plenty of quizzes online which will help you find out which you prefer if you are unsure. To learn successfully, we need to both 'do' and 'think' (or 'think' and 'do'). It is the combination of these two that enables learning to take place. Many learning theories break these two stages down further, allowing for doing, reflecting, concluding and planning. My preferred model is Plan-Do-Review, as people seem to remember this more easily.

You can start anywhere in this model; the important thing is that you follow it round in order to land each layer of learning. Below are examples of questions you can ask yourself on a regular basis to layer your learning from day to day experiences. You can change the questions depending on the context, but this should give you enough of a guide for you to be able to start using this format in your journaling. You don't need to answer each question – just those that resonate at the time. Since our brains can become lazy when asked the same questions each time, mix it up a little to keep finding new pearls of wisdom.

Plan, do, review

Plan

- What could you do next? What else?

- What would 'good' look like?

- What will you do more of?

- What will you do less of?

- What will you stop/start/continue doing?

- What can you do to get even more learning?

- What might get in the way? How could you overcome this?

- How committed are you to doing your actions?

- What are your intentions going forward?

- What do you want to think, do and know by the end of the next learning cycle?

Do

- What did you do? What actions did you take?

- What was driving those actions?

- Describe your mindset.

- What didn't you do that you intended to do?

- What impact did other people or things have on your actions?

Review

- What has changed as a result of your actions?

- What are you learning about yourself?

- What are you learning about others?

- What went well? Why?

- What didn't go so well? Why?

- What could you have done differently?

- What enabled you to take the actions you did?

- What got in the way of you doing more?

- What conclusions can you draw?

- What are you grateful for?

Find yourself a buddy

To accompany you on your learning journey, I highly recommend working with a buddy or accountability partner. In my experience, this is a significant factor in the success our clients experience. Buddying is a useful opportunity for leaders to support and challenge each other on their aspirations, impact, and alignment with company values and in bringing to life aspects of culture which the organisation is wishing to enhance.

Buddies get together virtually or face-to-face on a regular basis for the following reasons:

- To recognise, explore and embed informal learning from day to day experiences including, but not limited to, any development sessions

- To hold each other to account for the actions they said they would take

- To be a sounding board for each other

- To learn from each other by having different styles, motivators, perspectives and experiences – I recommend pairing up with someone very different from yourself

- To role model the behaviours associated with a learning culture: for example, prioritising learning, learning from mistakes and not just relying on formal training for learning to occur

- To practise the art of coaching (a vital skill for any leader)

Having a buddy also means that individuals make time for learning. A person is much more likely to commit to this time if they know that they are holding the space for someone else's growth too.

When having buddy sessions remember that this is a meeting in which it is vital that you show up with a present and grounded mindset. Having a structure of buddy conversations can also be useful (the Plan-Do-Review model is quick to understand, easy to apply and transferable to one-to-ones, project reviews and other areas where learning occurs).

Embedding

The CREATE model contains some techniques which will enable you to bring about sustainable and 'sticky' growth. The first is journaling. Writing ideas and intentions down on paper helps people think more deeply about what they want to achieve and why. It also leads to more action and greater commitment.

The second is measurability. When individuals know that they will be able to measure results (or more powerfully, others will be holding them to account for the results), they are more likely to follow through on their intentions. By having a detailed account of your Current Reality, you now have a benchmark which you can measure your success by. (If you have done a Motivational Map, you will also have measures around the extent to which you are motivated which can be measured again at any point in the future.)

A third way in which you can make learning stick is through sharing your experiences with others. We have covered this in the Engage part of the CREATE process and by encouraging you to have a buddy. Talking regularly about your aspirations, learnings, obstacles and successes reinforces the progress you are making and reminds your brain what to aim for.

A further aspect which can enhance how much learning is embedded is by involving your seniors. Knowing that people senior to you are taking an interest in your learning will greatly increase the likelihood of you applying it. If you don't have any immediate seniors (or don't respect the opinions of the ones that you do have), find yourself a mentor or simply grab a coffee with someone you admire and tell them about what you are up to.

Having access to experts is another way of embedding learning. This might be about having access to the trainers on the programme you went on, or to the peers you worked with on a project. I make sure I regularly network with experts to keep me on my toes, and ensure that I remain accessible to my clients to help them continually progress with their learning.

Summary

- Once you have completed the CREATE process, the next stages are Learn and Embed.

- Are you a 'doer' or a 'thinker'?

- Use Plan-Do-Review to layer your learning every day.

- Work with a buddy to enhance your learning even further.

- Make your learning stick by writing your aspirations down, checking in on measurable progress made, and sharing your experiences with peers, seniors and experts.

TEN

Conclusions And Next Steps

You now have the steps to CREATE the space to step into the best version of yourself as a leader. Investing in the process outlined in this book will offer real dividends over the coming months and years.

Current Reality

By dedicating time to exploring your Current Reality, you created a benchmark that you can look back on in future months to see what progress you have made. You updated your mindset to an accurate, current 'version' of yourself. You celebrated the skills, behaviours, knowledge and experience that helped you get to this point, and you started to understand why you bothered to apply yourself to these in the first place.

You identified the key outcomes you have delivered, noting the ones you are most proud of as well as the unhelpful behaviours and motivations that led to results you or others did not want.

Envisioning

Stepping into your future self gave you a glimpse of what can be; where your dreams become reality. This process may have felt 'other-worldly', a peek into the unknown; or it may have simply been a case of focusing your mind on that which is possible through careful extrapolation of what you already know. Whichever way you arrived at your envisioned future, I trust it was a good one. By holding this vision in your mind's eye and really associating each of your five senses with it, you can now bring a version of this future into existence.

Alignment

To experience congruence and ease, it is vital that the components of your envisioned future are in alignment. Your 'why bother' leads you to use and develop certain skills and behaviours effortlessly. Your 'why bother' shows you which direction to apply your energy. Your 'how' and your 'what' work in partnership – each feeding the other. This is a sustainable way of both working and leading as it adds energy to your reserves, rather than depleting them.

By having a clear understanding of what is important to you, you can look outside of yourself to build alignment with the teams and organisations in which you work. You will experience a better 'fit' between what you want and what they want. This means you are likely to stay within those environments for longer, contributing fully while receiving what you want and need from them. Symbiosis in action.

Test-out

With a positive tension between where you are and where you want to be, you may be keen to get going. The Test-out phase is a reminder that you will have a greater chance of ongoing success if you consider the potential twists and turns ahead. It is surprising how resourceful you can be when unfettered by the stress of being caught in an unexpectedly tricky situation. By resourcefully considering your options ahead of time you will see more choices available to you and make wiser decisions. By being open to new experiences and connections you will also be able to make the most of opportunities that come your way.

Engage

We are social beings. We were born to collaborate and work with others. We can realise our best selves when we work in an interdependent way, giving and receiving, challenging and supporting. Even the most self-aware person has blind spots, so we can all benefit from the cheerleading of our teams when we do well and the consolation, support and tough feedback when we fail. For fail we will. It is not possible to take strides towards our best version, to be the leaders this world needs, without taking a leap outside of our comfort zone – sometimes in doing so we will get it wrong. What sets true leaders apart is how they get up, brush themselves down, learn from their errors and show up better as a result. Learn to see failure as your friend and greatest teacher. This mindset will help you grow.

Learn and embed

The Learn phase of your journey is ever present. As long as you take the time to work your way through the learning cycle of Plan-Do-Review (from whichever point you like to start), you will continue to grow. Whether you journal your experiences daily (as I do) or talk them through with a coach, mentor or buddy frequently (as I also do), the important thing is to be deliberate about your learning.

Don't forget to celebrate. Catching yourself 'doing it right' provides real encouragement to keep going (keep growing), especially when you see it bringing your desired future into existence. Be a role model of this habit of positive reinforcement to others too and you might find it gets reciprocated.

Take stock of the progress you are making from time to time. Be mindful of what is enabling success and what the barriers along the way are. For the former, find ways to embed these practices so they become the new norm. For the latter, work with others to find ways to remove or work around them so they fall away.

Share your successes. If you have found the exercises in this book useful, recommend them to others. Coach, support and challenge each other to step into better versions of leadership. You will begin to see the difference you are making. Your newfound sense of clarity and conviction in what you are doing and the ease and grace in which you do it will make you stand out. Be ready to share how you have done it.

Circle around

Growth and expansion are not linear, nor can the future be predicted. Your aspirations for both will lead to actions that follow these intentions. As you approach the next vantage point on your journey through the mountain range, it is important to repeat the practice you now know will hold you in good stead. Circle back and take stock of your new Current Reality. Linger a while and consider what your next version of yourself will be. Be deliberate in finding internal alignment to this version and exploring how you will gain alignment with others. Test-out your options before Engaging with others. CREATE is a cyclical process; one which spirals upwards.

A new place to stand

My ambition is for people to have the clarity to cut through the many tasks that could be done and only do those which will make a difference. My hope is for people to step into their greatness deliberately: standing in a place that balances humility and a sense of self-worth enables us to be brave, courageous and generous in the work that we do. Having consistency and conviction and balancing support and challenge within a team enables its members to make the positive impact they seek.

At the beginning of this book I asked you to imagine standing in a different place. A place where you have real clarity, confidence and conviction in your role as a leader. Where you have harmony between your work and home life. Where you have alignment between what drives you and what drives the company you work for. Where everything you do feels focused and meaningful. Being so lost in your work, and in such a glorious state of flow that when you emerge you have achieved great things and feel energised. My hope is that you are now standing in that vantage point.

A final word

When individuals, and then teams, start to align their 'what', 'how' and 'why bother', they begin to generate a sustainable level of performance. As employees and customers alike begin to demand more from organisations in terms of the impact they have on the world, I believe we will see a deluge of organisations who genuinely place the pursuit of Purpose alongside profit. We will start to see the two-degree shift that is needed to bring about a different future. One in which employees love what they do and have their needs and wants consistently met at work, leaving them energised and ready to engage with family, friends, hobbies and other activities. Imagine the overall impact on personal well-being and society as a whole. As we consider our next steps as leaders, remember that by changing the paradigm around motivation in the workplace, we can bring about a better future for ourselves, our children and beyond. What will your motivators drive you to achieve?

Afterword

Towards and away from motivation

Over the last few years I have had an 'interesting' relationship with running. When I first started running (plodding would probably be more accurate), I was fed up with my post-maternity weight gain, fed up with how sluggish my body felt, and feeling uncomfortable in my clothes. My 'away from' motivation was clear. I wanted to be away from those feelings of heaviness, sluggishness and tightness. My 'towards' motivation was less clear. I wanted to feel better, but when tried to define what better looked like, I kept circling round to my 'away from' motivations. I just couldn't see myself able to run with ease, enjoying each step and getting a buzz from the whole experience. I didn't identify with those fabulous friends and colleagues of mine who ran marathons and half marathons. I told myself they were different to me. They were natural runners. They had more will power.

As the 'away from' motivation gained in strength, it eventually propelled me, compelled me to do something and so I started the NHS 'Couch to 5k' running programme. Slowly but surely, I started to run. On the cold winter days when running was the last thing I wanted to do, I reminded myself of my 'away from' motivators and I kept going. As I continued with my running, I noticed how free I felt. It was a time just for me, and as any parent of young children knows, those moments are rare. Freedom was added to my reasons for running, but this was still an 'away from' motivator. As the weeks and months passed, I managed to go further and further. This took longer and longer, and so my reward became both more freedom and more fitness. I reached a milestone of 7.7 miles (I'd meant to run 6.2 miles which is 10 kilometres but got my route wrong and decided to just keep running). It felt great. I had achieved, in fact smashed, a target. I concluded that unfit people can't run 10 kilometres plus and so I had to be fit. Then a strange thing happened. Over the next few weeks, my trainers had fewer outings. When I did dig them out, they plodded shorter distances, until I felt that I could no longer call myself a runner. What had happened? I still had the skills to run – in fact, more skills than at the beginning of my journey. My 'will' had simply gone.

We see this phenomenon all the time in the diet and fitness industry (it's often the cause of yo-yo dieting). When people have a strong 'away' motivation, when the pain is too much and doing nothing simply brings more pain, then they are compelled to act. They start moving in the direction which causes less pain, ie away from pain. When they eventually reach a stage where the pain is gone, or at least quietened sufficiently that it no longer impacts on them, they stop whatever was doing them good. They may benefit from the work done to date for a while, but they slowly slip back into old habits. They slip back towards the pain. Some may catch themselves and put those good habits back into action again, but if not caught in time, other voices can begin to crowd out motivation.

In my case, running was my 'away' motivation. As my pain eased, I began to slip back into old habits. My inner voices began to tell me, 'You can pick up running any time; right now you need to concentrate on moving; so what if you're overweight, just buy a new pair of jeans; skiing is ages way, do the running next year,' or worse still, 'you did all that work to get fit and you've slumped back here – now you know what you'll need to go through to get there so don't bother, 'cos you'll only end up here again...' Those gremlins have a lot to answer for! I decided to apply my CREATE model in my personal life to get me fit again. This time, I'm approaching it from the other end of the spectrum – the pleasure side. (If you're interested, watch how I get on in my blog: www.motivationalleadership.co.uk/blog)

References

Adams, A J, 'Seeing is Believing: The Power of Visualization', *Psychology Today*, 2009, www.psychologytoday.com/us/blog/flourish/200912/seeing-is-believing-the-power-visualization [accessed 13 February 2020].

Blanchard, K, 'Catch People Doing Something Right', not dated, www.kenblanchardbooks.com/catch-people-doing-something-right [accessed 13 February 2020].

Cameron, J, *The Artist's Way*, 1995, Pan Books, London.

Cashman, K, *Leadership from the Inside Out*, 2008, Berrett-Koehler Publishers, Oakland, CA.

Covey, S R, 'Big Rocks', not dated, www.youtube.com/watch?v=zV3gMTOEWt8 [accessed 13 February 2020].

Csikszentmihalyi, M, *Flow: The Psychology of Optimal Experience*, 2002, Rider, London.

Dweck, C, *Mindset*, 2017, Robinson, New York.

GALLUP, 'State of the Global Workplace', not dated, www.gallup.com/workplace/238079/state-global-workplace-2017.aspx [accessed 13 Feb 2020].

Goleman, D, *Emotional Intelligence: Why it can matter more than IQ*, 1996, Bloomsbury, London.

Jobs, S, commencement address delivered at Stanford University, 12 June 2005, https://news.stanford.edu/2005/06/14/jobs-061505 [accessed 13 February 2020].

Jung, C J, *The Psychology of Transference*, 1983, Routledge, London.

Lencioni, P, *The Five Dysfunctions of a Team*, 2002, John Wiley and Sons, New York.

Maraboli, S, *Life, the Truth, and Being Free*, 2009, A Better Today Publishing, New York.

Maslow, A, 'A Theory of Human Motivation', *Psychological Review*, 50(4), 1943, pp370–96.

Oliver, M, 'The Summer Day', *New and Selected Poems*, 1992, Beacon Press, Boston, MA.

Rogers, C, 'A theory of therapy, personality and interpersonal relationships as developed in the client-centered framework', in S. Koch (ed.), *Psychology: A study of a science, Vol 3: Formulation of the person and the social context*, 1959, McGraw-Hill, New York.

Sale, J, *Mapping Motivation: Unlocking the key to employee energy and engagement*, 2016, Gower, London.

Senge, P, *The Fifth Discipline*, 2006, Random House, London.

Sharma, R S, *The Leader Who Had No Title*, 2010, Simon and Schuster UK Ltd, UK.

Sinek, S, 'The Golden Circle', *TED Talks*, 2009, TEDx, Puget Sound, Washington, https://youtu.be/fMOlfsR7SMQ [accessed 13 February 2020].

Useful resources

Insights, www.insights.com

Motivational Leadership,
www.motivationalleadership.co.uk

Motivational Maps®, www.motivationalmaps.com

Myers Briggs, www.myersbriggs.org

Acknowledgements

I would like to thank the following people for their help during the writing of this book.

Dr Joanna Martin, Annie Stoker, Susie Heath and the wonderful ladies at OneofMany® without whom I would have not found the self-belief to write this book in the first place.

Jenny Leeming, The Business Whisperer, whose patience, structure, insight and support led to the birth of this book.

Lynne Bell, my fellow founding director at Motivational Leadership, who believed I 'had a book in me' years before I realised it. Thank you for cheering me on.

Verity Ridgman, Caroline Prodger and the team at Rethink Press who have expertly guided me through the book writing process and made it a joy.

Holly Pither from TribePR who has been a recent but important addition to the Motivational Leadership team and helping us build our brand.

Bridget Siddle for continuing to be a joy to work with and in whom I trust to run the business whilst I write and play.

James and Linda Sale at Motivational Maps® Limited. Maps is such a great tool and your books, James, have given me the insight I needed to be able to build my own ideas. Thank you for your continued support.

To our growing team of Mappers (Licensed Practitioners) who already know what power harnessing motivation can have in businesses. I hope this book gives you even more ideas to help your clients build purposeful and profitable companies.

Julie Woodman, Veronica Reed, Ali Stewart, Helen Schick and Sue Price for their valuable feedback during the writing process - and beyond. And double thanks to Ali for you have inspired me with your book writing – texts which now contribute so much to our business.

The many teams that I have had the privilege to have worked with over the years especially those who have embraced the importance of motivation including Alzheimer's Society, RSPCA, John Lewis and Partners, Novartis, Bargate Homes, National Housing Federation, The National Lottery Community Fund, Oxford Said Business School and many more.

To my fellow collaborators Claire Osborn, Julia Carter, Carole Gaskell, Joy Burnford and Caroline Gosling all of whom are making a huge difference in the world of leadership and I learn so much from every time we speak.

And of course to Maisie and Amelie who have kept me on track and inspired me to write a book I hope they can be proud of.

The Author

Kate is the founding Director of Motivational Leadership and a leading expert in Motivational Maps® in the UK. Kate's ambition is to change the paradigm around motivation in the workplace. She believes that enabling people to gain a better understanding of what drives them allows them to take responsibility for, and ultimately increase, their own level of motivation, engagement and performance. Aligning this awareness to the opportunities available ensures that peoples' skills remain relevant throughout their career. Kate recognises that when you get motivation right, not only do you drive up performance, productivity and return on investment, but you also drive up well-being, happiness, and positively impact the human experience.

Contact us through our website: www.motivationalleadership.co.uk or email us at info@motivationalleadership.co.uk

We have created several free resources to help you to turn some of the ideas in this book into reality: www.create-motivation.co.uk/resources

Our blog is also full of extra information and additional resources: www.motivationalleadership.co.uk/blog

I am also on social media and would love to be in contact with you on LinkedIn:

in www.linkedin.com/in/kateturner1